线条艺术的遗产

唐乾陵陪葬墓石椁线刻画

樊英峰　王双怀

文物出版社

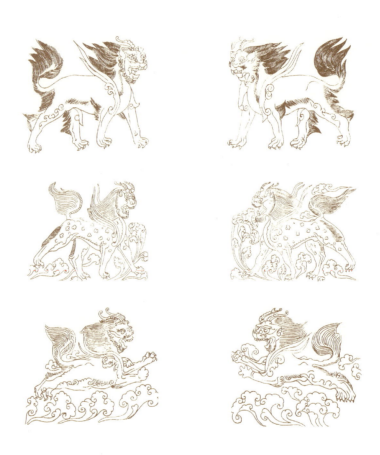

《线条艺术的遗产》编辑委员会

编委会主任：景雪峰

副主任：樊英峰　王双怀

编　委：丁　伟　陈占地　陈彦德　王志孝
　　　　刘　茜　王平义　刘向阳　王晓莉
　　　　侯晓斌　宋小龙　曾晓琦　张　鑫

策划指导：葛承雍

编著者：樊英峰　王双怀

绘　图：侯晓斌　董守信

摄　影：田　园

资料整理：李青峰　穆兴平　魏　鹏　郑　勋
　　　　　刘　艳　杨麦娟　李阿能　赵维娜
　　　　　吕　涛　李育红

英文翻译：杨金梅

日文翻译：曹　婷

前　言　　　　　　　　　　　　　　　　　　　　014

第一编
章怀太子墓石椁线刻画　　　　　　　　　　　045

第一节　章怀墓石椁线刻画布局　　　　　　　　047
   Ⅰ　外部画面　　　　　　　　　　　　　　047
   Ⅱ　内部画面　　　　　　　　　　　　　　049

第二节　章怀墓石椁外部线刻画　　　　　　　　052
   Ⅰ　外柱线刻画　　　　　　　　　　　　052
   Ⅱ　外壁线刻画　　　　　　　　　　　　068

第三节　章怀墓石椁内部线刻画　　　　　　　　095
   Ⅰ　内柱线刻画　　　　　　　　　　　　095
   Ⅱ　内壁线刻画　　　　　　　　　　　　097

第四节　章怀墓线刻画题材要素　　　　　　　　117
   Ⅰ　人物　　　　　　　　　　　　　　　117
   Ⅱ　动物　　　　　　　　　　　　　　　118
   Ⅲ　植物　　　　　　　　　　　　　　　120

第二编
懿德太子墓石椁线刻画　　　　　　　　　　　123

第一节　懿德墓石椁线刻画布局　　　　　　　　125
   Ⅰ　外部画面　　　　　　　　　　　　　125
   Ⅱ　内部画面　　　　　　　　　　　　　126

第二节　懿德墓石椁外部线刻画　　　　　　　　130
   Ⅰ　外柱线刻画　　　　　　　　　　　　130
   Ⅱ　外壁线刻画　　　　　　　　　　　　141

第三节 懿德墓石椁内部线刻画   156

ⅠⅠ 内柱线刻画   156

ⅠⅠ 内壁线刻画   164

第四节 懿德墓线刻画题材要素   184

Ⅰ 人物   184

Ⅱ 动物   188

Ⅲ 植物   192

第三编
永泰公主墓石椁线刻画   203

第一节 永泰墓石椁线刻画布局   204

Ⅰ 外部画面   206

Ⅱ 内部画面   208

第二节 永泰墓石椁外部线刻画   210

Ⅰ 外柱线刻画   210

Ⅱ 外壁线刻画   220

第三节 永泰墓石椁内部线刻画   234

Ⅰ 内柱线刻画   234

Ⅱ 外壁线刻画   242

第四节 永泰墓线刻画题材要素   262

Ⅰ 人物   262

Ⅱ 动物   266

Ⅲ 植物   268

后 记   271

Preface   023

Chapter 1.
Line Engravings on the Stone Outer Coffin of
The Zhanghuai Prince Tomb   045

Section 1. Layout of the or Engravings on the Zhanghuai Prince Tomb's Stone Outer Coffin   047

❶   Exterior Line Engrewings   047

❷   Interior Line Engrewings   049

Section 2.   Engravings on the Exterior Surface of the Zhanghuai Prince Tomb's Stone Outer Coffin   052

❶   Engravings on the Exterior Columns   052

❷   Engravings on the Exterior Walls   068

Section 3.   Engravings on the Interior Surface of the Zhanghuai Prince Tomb's Stone Outher Coffin   095

❶   Engravings on the Interior Columns   095

❷   Engravings on the Interior Walls   097

Section 4. Key Elements of the Themes of the Zhanghuai Prince Prince Tomb's Engravings   117

❶   Characters   117

❷   Animals   118

❸   Plants   120

Chapter 2.
Line Engravings on the Stone Outer Coffin of
The Yide Prince Tomb   123

Section 1. Layout of the Engravings on the Yide Prince Tomb's Stone Outer Coffin   125

❶   Exterior Frames   125

❷   Interior Frames   126

Section 2.   Engravings on the Exterior Surface of the Yide Prince Tomb's Stone Outer Coffin   130

❶   Engravings on the Exterior Columns   130

❷   Engravings on the Exterior Walls   141

Section 3. Engravings on the Interior Surface of the Yide Prince Tomb's Stone Outer Coffin 156

❶   Engravings on the Interior Columns   156

❷   Engravings on the Interior Walls   164

Preface   007

Section 4. Key Elements of the Themes of the Yide Princess Tomb's Engravings   184

     Ⅰ   Characters   184

     Ⅱ   Animals   188

     Ⅲ   Plants   192

Chapter 3.
Line Engravings on the Stone Outer Coffin of
The Yongtai Princess Tomb   203

Section 1. Layout of the Engravings on the Yongtai Tomb's Princess Stone Outer Coffin   204

     Ⅰ   Exterior Frames   206

     Ⅱ   Interior Frames   208

Section 2.   Engravings on the Exterior Surface of the Yongtai Princess Tomb's Stone Outer Coffin   210

     Ⅰ   Engravings on the Exterior Columns   210

     Ⅱ   Engravings on the Exterior Walls   220

Section 3.   Engravings on the Interior Surface of the Yongtai Princess Tomb's Stone Outrr Coffin   234

     Ⅰ   Engravings on the Interior Columns   242

     Ⅱ   Engravings on the Interior Walls   262

Section 4. Key Elements of the Themes of the Yongtai Princess Tomb's Engravings   262

     Ⅰ   Characters   262

     Ⅱ   Animals   266

     Ⅲ   Plants   268

Postscript   271

まえがき　　035

第一章　章懐太子墓の石槨における石刻線画　　045

第一節　章懐太子墓の石槨における石刻線画の構成　　047

　Ⅰ　外側の画面　　047

　Ⅱ　内側の画面　　049

第二節　章懐太子墓の石槨における外側の石刻線画　　052

　Ⅰ　外部の柱に刻まれている石刻線画　　052

　Ⅱ　外壁に刻まれている石刻線画　　068

第三節　章懐太子墓の石槨における内側の石刻線画　　095

　Ⅰ　内部の柱に刻まれている石刻線画　　095

　Ⅱ　内壁に刻まれている石刻線画　　097

第四節　章懐太子墓における石刻線画の題材　　117

　Ⅰ　人物　　117

　Ⅱ　動物　　118

　Ⅲ　植物　　120

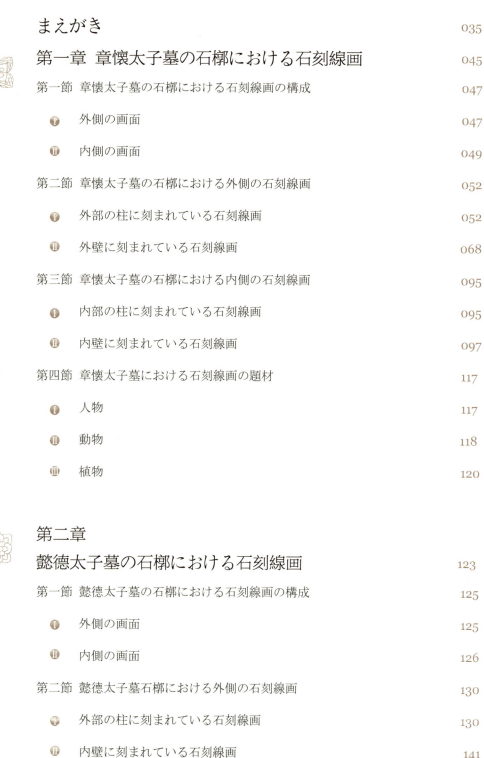
第二章
懿徳太子墓の石槨における石刻線画　　123

第一節　懿徳太子墓の石槨における石刻線画の構成　　125

　Ⅰ　外側の画面　　125

　Ⅱ　内側の画面　　126

第二節　懿徳太子墓石槨における外側の石刻線画　　130

　Ⅰ　外部の柱に刻まれている石刻線画　　130

　Ⅱ　内壁に刻まれている石刻線画　　141

第三節　懿徳太子墓の石槨における内側の石刻線画　156

　　❶　内部の柱に刻まれている石刻線画　156

　　❷　内壁に刻まれている石刻線画　164

第四節　懿徳太子墓における石刻線画の題材　184

　　❶　人物　184

　　❷　動物　188

　　❸　植物　192

第三章
永泰公主墓の石槨における石刻線画　203

第一節　永泰公主墓の石槨における石刻線画の構成　204

　　❶　外側の画面　206

　　❷　内側の画面　208

第二節　永泰公主墓の石槨における外側の石刻線画　210

　　❶　外部の柱に刻まれている石刻線画　210

　　❷　外壁に刻まれている石刻線画　220

第三節　永泰公主墓の石槨における内側の石刻線画　234

　　❶　内部の柱に刻まれている石刻線画　234

　　❷　内壁に刻まれている石刻線画　242

第四節　永泰公主墓における石刻線画の題材　262

　　❶　人物　262

　　❷　動物　266

　　❸　植物　268

あとがき　271

乾陵夕照

乾陵神道

乾陵陪葬墓

前　言

　　乾陵是唐高宗李治和女皇帝武则天的合葬墓。这座陵墓规模宏大，气势磅礴，被誉为"关中唐陵之冠"。目前，乾陵地宫尚未发掘，但考古工作者从陪葬的章怀太子墓、永泰公主墓和懿德太子墓中，出土了大量文物，其中包括不少精美的石刻线画。所谓石刻线画就是用镌刻技法在石版上绘制的画作。由于这种画作主要是用线条在石版上钩勒出来的，因此，人们在习惯上称之为"线刻画"或"石刻画"。这种画作不同于画在纸上的绘画作品，不同于画在墙上的壁画，不同于画在岩上的岩画，也不同于画在或刻在木版上的版画，"是我国艺苑中特有的一种艺术"[1]。从历史和现实的角度来看，乾陵陪葬墓石刻线画的艺术价值与史料价值十分突出，是唐代石刻艺术的杰作，具有永恒的魅力，值得我们进行深入研究。

一

　　乾陪葬墓石刻线画是唐代石刻线画的重要组成部分，而唐代的石刻线画则是在前代石刻线画的基础上发展起来的。因此，可以说唐代陪葬墓石刻线画在一定程度上受到了前代的影响。

　　有资料表明，中国石刻线画源远流长，可以追溯到先秦时期。考古工作者发现的一些史前时期的岩画，即带有石刻线画的性质。商周时期的石棺石椁上，已经有了石刻线画的痕迹。秦汉时期是中国石刻线画发展的第一个高峰。这一时期石刻线画的主要形式是画像砖和画像石。其形式多为减底浅雕，内容则以鬼神世界和人间生活为主。1980年在山东嘉祥宋山村出土的汉代画像石就是如此。该画像石分为四层，上层表现神界鬼域，刻绘西王母、仙人和精灵；下层表现现实生活，刻绘官宦人物；中间两层则刻绘"季杞挂剑"、"二桃杀三士"等历史故事。汉代画像石棺一般分布于砖室墓或崖墓之中[2]。西汉早期的画像石棺，多刻画门阙、树木、人物等，内容相对较简单。西汉晚期，石椁墓增多，内容也趋于丰富，除表现现实生活的出行、狩猎、乐舞形象外，还出现了伏羲、女娲、西王母等传说人物和神仙鬼怪的形象。如山东邹城县博物馆收藏的出土于郭里镇的石椁，就刻有雷公、雨师、

西王母等神仙。到了东汉，画像石臻于全盛，考古工作者在四川、山东、河南、陕西、内蒙等地发现了大量的画像石，其内容涉及神仙鬼怪、市井生活、历史故事、装饰纹样等诸多方面，达到较高的艺术水平。

　　魏晋南北朝时期，佛教的发展给石刻线画注入了新的活力。这一时期，画像砖、画像石趋于衰落，佛教造像方兴未艾。在一些重要的佛教造像上，往往刻画有佛本生故事、佛传故事或佛教故事。如陕西历史博物馆收藏的北魏皇兴五年（471）造像分为七层，自上而下，以连环画的形式，刻画佛传故事。到了隋唐时期，石刻线画仍保持着发展的势头。这一时期的石刻线画主要盛行于两个领域：一是宗教界，一是陵墓中。前者继魏晋南北朝之余续，因佛教和道教的繁荣而发展。大雁塔门楣上的"说法图"和天尊像座上的供养道士图即是宗教石刻线画的代表。后者则因石椁墓葬和墓志碑刻的兴起而繁荣。

　　唐代墓葬中的石刻线画主要分布在石门的门楣、门扇和棺椁的内外两侧。有学者认为，这是唐代墓葬图像系统的"固定格式"，具有普遍的象征意义[3]。从考古资料和实际观察的情况来看，乾陵陪葬墓石刻线画的载体是石门和石椁。其石料可能采自陕西富平玉镜山，均经过精心打磨加工处

[1] 王树村：《中国石刻线画略史》，刊《中国美术全集·绘画编》19，上海人民出版社1988年，第1页。
[2] 张孜江：《两汉时期的画像石棺石椁艺术》，《文物鉴定与鉴赏》2011年第8期，第20页。

理，大小形制根据石门和石椁的实际需要而定。线画即镌刻在石门的门楣、门扇，石椁的内外倚柱和厢板上。乾陵至少有十七座陪葬墓，目前已经发掘了五座，即章怀太子墓、懿德太子墓、永泰公主墓、李谨行墓和薛元超墓。考古工作者在这些墓葬中发现了不少石刻线画。本书只对章怀太子墓、懿德太子墓和永泰公主墓石椁上的线刻画进行了整理。

二

章怀太子墓、懿德太子墓和永泰公主墓都是在唐中宗神龙元年（705）至神龙二年修建的。由于下葬的时间大体相同，因而墓葬的制度和规模颇为相似，但由于章怀太子、懿德太子和永泰公主的身份地位有所不同，其墓葬形制也存在着一些差异。这种情况在石椁的线刻画上也有所体现。

章怀太子李贤是高宗李治和武则天的第二个儿子，上元二年(675)六月三日立为太子。调露元年（679）、仪凤四年（679）年间曾奉命监国。撰有

《春宫要录》十卷[4]，《列藩正论》三十卷[5]，《修身要录》十卷[6]，并曾为《后汉书》作注。永隆元年（680），因李贤私藏皂甲"谋逆"被废李贤为庶人，开耀元年（681）十一月八日，流放到巴州幽禁。文明元年二月廿七日，在巴州公馆自杀，死时年仅三十一岁。垂拱元年（685）被武则天追封为"雍王"。神龙二年（706）迁葬陪陵。墓园南北长180米，东西宽143米，面积25740平方米。封土呈覆斗形，高约18米。1971年至1972年，考古人员对此墓进行了发掘，出土文物600多件。石椁位于后墓室，由33块青石板组成，长3.745米，宽2.85米，高1.85米。其内外柱及内外壁均有精美的线刻画，数量达40幅之多。

懿德太子李重润是唐高宗和武则天之嫡孙、唐中宗与韦皇后之长子。开耀二年生于东宫内殿。永淳元年（682）被立为皇太孙。文明元年（684）因中宗被废而成为庶人。圣历初（698）中宗复立为皇太子时被封为邵王。大足元年（701）九月，因与其妹永泰郡主及主婿魏王武延基等窃议张易之兄弟入宫之事，为张易

章怀太子墓石椁线刻画尺寸统计表
单位：厘米

规格		第一幅	第二幅	第三幅	第四幅	第五幅	第六幅	第七幅	第八幅	第九幅	第十幅	第十一幅	第十二幅	第十三幅	第十四幅
内柱	长	136	137	135	136	137	136								
	宽	35	33	32	35	34	30								
外柱	长	137	135	133.5	137	136	133	137	138	134	136	135	138	136	138
	宽	36	34	34	34	33	33	34	30	35	33.5	35.5	34	31	36
内壁	长	126	128	131	130	130	125	125	125	124	124				
	宽	80	75	69	81	68	79	83	74	67	73				
外壁	长	131	130	132	131	132	127	128	132	130	133				
	宽	81	75	67	80	63	74	81	74	68	69				
备注	顺序从西北开始顺时针起始														

[1] 李星明：《唐代墓室壁画研究》，陕西人民美术出版社2005年，第138页
[3] 《新唐书》卷59《艺文志三》，页1509
[4] 《新唐书》卷58《艺文志二》，页1480
[5] 《旧唐书》卷47《经籍志下》，页2026

之所逼。武则天让中宗严查，结果被杖杀，年仅19岁，葬于洛阳。中宗复位后，追赠为懿德太子，于神龙二年（706）迁葬，以帝王之礼陪葬乾陵。墓园长256.5米，宽214米，面积54891平方米。封土呈覆斗形，高17.92米。经1971年至1972年发掘，发现后墓室之大型石椁。石椁长3.7米，宽2.82米，高1.87米。内外部倚柱及椁壁上有精美线刻画33幅。

永泰公主李仙蕙为唐高宗与武则天之孙女，为唐中宗与韦后所生。久视元年（700）被封为永泰郡主，食邑一千户，嫁给魏王武延基。大足元年（701）因窃议张易之等入宫事，被迫自杀，年仅17岁，葬于洛阳。中宗复位后于神龙元年（705年）追赠"永泰公主"，令有司备礼改葬。次年迁葬陪陵，与其夫武延基合窆。1960年至1964年，考古工作者对其墓进行了科学发掘，出土了大量文物。其石椁长3.77米，宽2.79米，高近两米，内外柱、壁有精美线刻画33幅。

上述三座陪葬墓的椁体量都比较大。内外壁每幅石刻线画面积一般为0.8-1.1平方米之间，内外柱的面积则为0.44平方米左右。厢板画刻人物（仕女、仆从）、动物（飞鸟、走兽）、植物（花卉、蔓草）和无生物（石头、建筑、器物等），是石刻线画的主体；倚柱画则刻蔓草、折枝、花卉、祥鸟、瑞兽等等，带有装饰的性质。

三

考察乾陵陪葬墓石刻线画，我们可以清楚地看到，人物及人物活动的元素是最主要的内容。在这里，我们以章怀太子墓的内外壁石刻线画为例。章怀太子墓石刻人物有14幅，刻画人物21个，全部为立像，神情姿态各异。当时奉行"视死如生"的丧葬理念，石刻线画主要表现墓主人生前的生活场景。

石椁内侧南壁线刻由西向东算起，第一幅石刻线画上有侍女二人。左一螺髻，簪钗，右一人凤钗。二人姿态一致，抄手伫立。有花三本，中间一株类似栀子花，左右两侧形似扶桑。右下侧有拳石。上部有山雀一只，作飞翔状。边饰为卷叶。第二幅石刻线画上有侍女二人，侧立，方向一致。前者为螺髻，后者为双螺髻。二人服饰相同，抄手伫立。中有大理菊类植物一株，高与目齐，枝叶错落有致。左边山葵类植物一株，上有双蝶飞舞。鸟二，一为杜鹃，一为山鹧。边饰缠枝海石榴。西壁由南至北算起，第一幅石刻线画上有侍女一人，抄手伫立，身材瘦削。螺髻，披巾，长裙曳地，云头鞋。左侧石柟花类植物一株，高与目齐。右

懿德太子墓石椁线刻画尺寸统计表
单位：厘米

	规格	第一幅	第二幅	第三幅	第四幅	第五幅	第六幅	第七幅	第八幅	第九幅	第十幅
内柱	长	133	134	134	133.5	133.5	134				
	宽	34	34	34	33	34	34				
外柱	长	135	134	134.5	134	134	135	134	134	134	135
	宽	34	34	34.5	34.3	34.5	35	30.5	34	35	34
内柱	长	131	130.5	127.5	128	129	131	131.5	131	129	129
	宽	80	79	68	74	68.5	80	80.5	66	72	68
外柱	长	130	129	136.5	133.5	133.5	131.5	130			
	宽	80.5	79	67	75.5	69.5	80	80			
备注	顺序从西北开始顺时针起始										

侧类似杜若一株，头上有飞鸟二：一为燕珩，一为杜鹃。左上侧有一蜻蜓。边花为大卷叶，系剔底线刻。第二幅上有侍女二人，左一螺髻，簪珠花，步摇，云头鞋，面部雍容妍丽，抄手伫立，若有所思。右一人双髻，圆领花袍，系腰带荷包，女扮男装，手捧包袱。中有金盏菊类植物一本，高过人体，花盛开。右侧近似红蓼一本，高与人等。右侧形似秋葵，下方太湖石一块，画百合花一朵，紫花地丁二株。头上有白头翁鸟一对，展翅高飞。第三幅为双髻侍女，头簪珠花，圆领衫，长裙曳地，绣鞋，双手捧盆景，内植山葵一株。上部有蜂蝶、蜻蜓飞舞。锦雀三只，展翅翱翔。右下窠石一块，黄花（金针花）一朵。左为金盏花一朵。北壁第一幅为一侍女，直立凝思，螺髻，面部端庄，体态轻盈，双手抄胸前，绣鞋，头脚均与边框线连接，显得身材修长。左侧类似茶花一株，右侧山葵一株，一杆直上，叶互生。上部两侧山鹧一对，边饰大卷叶纹。第二幅亦为侍女一人，螺髻，抄手伫立，披巾搭于双手上，长袍曳地，云头鞋。左有锦葵一本，高齐人目。一杆直上，顶部花二苞。右侧萱花一株，一花三蕾。萱花之上，刻茶花一株。右上侧刻一鸠飞翔。边饰大卷叶，系剔底凸面叶瓣。东壁第一幅为侍女一人，双手托花钵，作花下承露状。螺髻，双目凝视一正开花朵。披巾搭于左肩上，衣

纹直立下垂。左为芙蓉一株，右为连翘一株。下有矾石，小草一株。上部中间一飞蝶，两侧各有黄雀一只，正凌空飞翔。边饰卷叶石榴。侍女一，头戴凤冠，两髻侧簪有步摇。花上衣，披巾，长裙。绣鞋，抄手伫立。背景为花石，左为木槿花一株，花正开，右为白芷花，下为拳石。人物上部两侧，有鸳鸯二只，飞向一致。

石椁外侧南壁第一幅有侍女二人，前右一螺髻，面庞丰满，花上衣，长披巾，长裙曳地，抄手侧立，神态端庄。后一人螺髻，女扮男装。翻领长袍，双手捧一雕花钵。系腰带，佩刀，较前一人低一头，似为侍从。中间木芙蓉一本，花正开。左上侧飞鸟一，形似鸠。边饰大叶海石榴。第二幅变有侍女二人。前者蝶形高髻，披巾，长裙曳地，侧身俯视，凝目观花。左手扶杆，右手折花枝。身材修长，体态绰约。后者女扮男装，翻领绣袍，幞头，手执一花，侧身作嗅花状，意态悠闲。下有块石，花三株，左侧一辛夷，高与人等，花盛开。人物身后有锦葵一本，与辛夷齐，有花有蕾，形势自然。边饰卷叶海石榴。东侧第一幅为庑殿门南窗棂。花纹分三部分。上为一对翼马，相对奔驰，以二株卷叶纹相间。中为直棂窗，有窗棂10根，四周以草叶纹饰。其下为二猛虎相对而立，张牙舞爪，欲作搏斗状。中以草叶纹相间，下为卷叶纹。第二幅象

永泰公主墓石椁线刻画尺寸统计表
单位：厘米

	规格	第一幅	第二幅	第三幅	第四幅	第五幅	第六幅	第七幅	第八幅	第九幅	第十幅
内柱	高	132	131.5	132.5	133.5	133	132.5				
	宽	35	35.5	35.5	35.3	35.5	35				
外柱	高	135	134.5	135	135	134	134	134	136	136	134
	宽	35.5	35	35	35	35.5	35	33.5	33.5	35.5	34.5
内柱	高	131.5	134.5	135	130.5	132.5	130.5	130.5	135.5	130.5	126
	宽	76.5	80	67.5	79	66	78	76	76	78	58.5
外柱	高	136.5	137	136.5	136	136	136	136			
	宽	76.5	80	68.5	80	66	77.5	76.5			
备注	顺序从西北开始顺时针起始，即第一幅为石椁西北第一张，依次类推。（下表同）										

征殿门，有枋额，门楣，上刻卷叶海石榴纹，舞凤一对，衔花枝，尾部转化为海石榴叶，四周边饰海石榴花纹。双扇，门上横饰花泡钉4排，每排7个。门中铺首衔环。门前侍卫二人。左宦官，右侍女。宦官折腰执笏，方脸颧高，戴幞头，两下角垂为党耳。侍女体肥硕，高髻，披巾，云头鞋，一臂下垂，手持披巾，作欲语之状。第三幅为殿门右窗。纹饰与左窗同。唯下部饰虎形物一对，头有角，似为獬豸之属。北侧第一幅一人，女扮男装，戴花冠，圆领长袍，正面，双手捧一方形包袱。上部有鸟、蝶。左侧为阔叶蜀葵。右为苍术一本，高度略与人齐。下部太湖石，边饰大叶卷草。第二幅，二侍女相对而立。左一双螺髻，圆领袍，手执彩绘盆。右一人高螺髻，披巾，一手举起，一手下垂，长裙，云头鞋。中间一花一树。花似山茶，叶似冬青。上栖画眉鸟一只，上方左右各有一鸟，正飞翔。左为黄鹂，右为青鸟。四周有折枝花四，右为郁金、锦葵，左为山茶、百合。下方勾勒山石，边饰大卷叶纹。

显然，以章怀太子墓人物画为代表的乾陵陪葬墓石刻线画显示了墓主人煊赫的身份和生前宫闱的华丽，展现了当时宫廷的生活场景，反映了当时宫廷上层社会的生活时尚和审美情趣。值得注意的是，在乾陵陪葬墓石刻线画的画面中，动物和植物也占有较大的比重，飞龙、舞凤、天马、麒麟、狮子、驼鸟、鸳鸯、仙鹤、异兽及各式花草都是相当醒目的。虽然它们在人物画中主要是起到一种装饰衬托的作用，但和画中姿态各异的人物和谐统一，成为整个画面不可或缺的一部分。

四

唐代石椁人物线刻是"白描"的一种传译形式[7]。其作者分为两类：一类是线刻样稿创作者，另一类是依据样稿施工的勒石工匠。乾陵陪葬墓石刻线画的镌刻方法大体有两种形式：

一种是线刻，另一种是减地线刻。大体来说，厢板石刻线画多采用细线阴刻的方法，直接以刀阴刻出线纹。这种线刻具有白描画或"铁线描"的风格。减地线刻又称"剔底线刻"，即沿花纹外廓将石面表层剔去，使花纹部分凸起，然后再于轮廓内以线条阴刻。至于具体的画刻过程，从章怀墓石椁西壁有所反映。石椁西壁一般地紧贴于后室西墙，因此石椁西壁外的线刻比较潦草、粗糙，有的因紧贴于西墙，因此根本就无法弄清它是否有石刻线画。如永泰石椁西壁即紧贴于后室西墙，二者之间的距离仅15厘米至20厘米左右。因积土无法清除，也就无从知晓椁外西壁是否有石刻线画。但是章怀墓石椁西壁与后室西墙之间尚有50厘米左右的距离，可容一人往来。总的来说，椁外西壁本不拟给人观看，因此，刻的粗犷潦草，简单，甚至连当时用白垩土涂底的白粉也保留未动，尚有几处留下了当初加工的痕迹。这种情况印证了《酉阳杂俎》中记载的线刻方法，是研究唐代石刻艺术的重要资料。就墓中石刻与同时期的一些墓中的线刻比较，我们可以得知，当时这些精心的雕饰，是先将青石或汉白玉石表面打磨光洁，然后以轻胶拌白垩土，用毛笔醮着在石面上起样，用刻刀刻出极轻细的线条作为稿子。稿子确定后，即一次镌刻而成。从刀痕与笔迹判断，有些地方是出自一人手笔，也有的是一人画稿，另一人镌刻。《酉阳杂俎》卷五载："平康坊菩提寺中，雕饰奇巧，相传郑法士所起样也"。郑法士为唐代壁画高手，与吴道子、卢楞伽齐名。他们为石刻雕饰起样，说明线刻在唐代是很受重视的一种艺术形式。

著名艺术史专家王树村先生认为，以往"绘刻石上的线画作品，多是出自民间艺人士"。[8]乾陵陪葬墓石刻线画的作者是谁？文献中没有明确记载。但乾陵墓主或为亲王，或为公主，身份特殊。从线

[7]李杰：《唐"白描"辨》，《艺术教育》2011年第1期。

刻画的内容来看，画中的人物大多是以现实人物为原型的，人物的胖瘦、大小也是与其身份地位相关联的。石刻线画的作者对墓主人的生活应当有一定的了解，这绝不是等闲之辈所能做到的。因此，画稿极有可能出自宫廷画师之手，而刻工也极有可能是雕刻者中的高手。就石刻线画本身而言，确实已经达到了很高的艺术水平。

乾陵陪葬墓石刻线画造型生动逼真，线纹流畅柔和，看上去十分美观。如章怀太子墓椁内的一幅石刻线画中，一侍女梳蝶形高髻，身着披巾，长裙曳地，左手扶杆，右手作攀折花枝状，侧身俯视，凝目观花，体态绰约；另一侍女女扮男装，着翻领绣袍，手执一花，侧身作嗅花状，仪态悠闲。又如永泰公主墓石椁内壁北边一幅"披巾侍女图"，画中侍女梳螺髻，簪步摇，上短襦，外半臂，两襟结于胸前，下着曳地长裙，柳眉凤眼，樱桃小口，一副亭亭玉立的少女形象。双手托起披巾，似欲翩翩而舞，静止的画面颇有几分动感。侍女的服饰也特有特点。有的梳单螺髻，有的梳双螺髻，还有梳单刀髻，戴幞头的。有的上短襦，外披巾，下着曳地长裙，脚着云头高履；有的穿翻领长袍，条纹裤，脚穿线鞋，腰系革带，并缀有饰品。再如懿德太子墓石椁外东壁石门上的一幅石刻线画中，两侍女盛装打扮，她们头戴凤冠，身着宫衣，相向抄手而立，似在为墓主人值夜。侍女周围亦有植物花卉点缀，门框四周饰以卷叶纹。门楣上是相向而舞的双凤，整个画面看起来富丽美观。这些石刻线画都很细致，具有流畅、刚劲、明快的特点。工匠在刻画时运笔稳健，压力均匀，线条粗细变化很小，显得含蓄秀劲，流畅自如，达到以线造型、形随线生、神随线出的艺术效果。根据画面的内容，所描绘的人物性格，或柔媚如丝，或刚劲似铁，不一而足。在构图上，按照主次分明、协调对称和整齐划一的原则安排内容，既突出了完整的画面，也显示了

工整的图案，使整个画面清晰严整富有生活气息，而又不显得复杂累赘。

唐人张彦远在《历代名画记》中说："无线者非画也"。由此可见线条对于绘画是何等重要。据研究，唐代画家在用笔实践中发展了中国传统的"高古游丝描"，善于表现含蓄连绵的"铁线描"和起伏变化的"兰叶描"，为中国画笔法的"描法"体系做出了不朽的贡献。[9] "铁线描"画法在魏晋南北朝之际已经产生，主要表现衣装褶纹，因线条粗细均匀，遒劲有力，状如"屈铁盘丝"，故有"铁线描"之称。这种画法在唐代得到很大发展，代表性的作品有阎立本的《历代帝王像》等。所绘帝王之衣服、胡须皆用铁线描画，形象逼真，可谓上乘之作。唐代墓室壁画，特别是棺椁石刻线画中，也经常使用"铁线描"。如永泰公主墓石椁上所刻宫女，或执纨扇，或捧玉盘，或端妆奁，或抱饭盒，或举烛台，举止娴静，仪容温顺，风姿卓约，造型优美，所著裙带，多用铁线描出，弯如曲铁，圆如盘丝，飘逸流畅，甚称石刻仕女画之杰作。"兰叶描"的特点是线型呈多种变化，压力不均，运笔时提高时顿，忽粗忽细，状如兰叶，故称"兰叶描"。据说这种画法是由唐代大画家吴道子创立的。吴道子常用此画法描摹人物，线条动荡，自由奔放，有"吴带当风"之说。

作为唐代绘画的重要组成部分，乾陵陪葬墓石刻线画是以线条为主的。其表现手法与传统中国画的白描手法极为相似，但它是以素净的线条架构画面，用线条造型描绘雕刻作品。石刻线画的特点是以石料为载体，以刀代笔，用线作画。故带有绘画和雕塑的双重性质。只有熟悉绘画艺术，又掌握雕刻技巧的人，才能完成这种工作。从乾陵陪葬墓石刻线画来看，当时的画家能够熟练地运用线条表现复杂的内容，而雕刻者亦能在线条与物形的紧密联系中表现线条的粗细、轻重、力度、质感、起伏、节奏、变化，当简则

王树村：《石刻线画之发展及其研究价值》，《美术史研究》2007年第3期，第68页。
陈授祥：《隋唐绘画史》，人民美术出版社2001年

简，当繁即繁，以境取线，以意取线，从而达到妙趣横生，超越自然的境界。

五

乾陵陪葬墓石刻线画不仅仅是一种艺术品，同时也是一种具有重要历史价值的文物。它保存了唐代前期一些著名画工和雕刻家的真迹，为我们提供了不少唐代历史文化方面的重要信息。

首先，它是我们研究唐代绘画的重要依据。唐代是我国绘画艺术蓬勃发展的时期。在唐代289年中，曾出一大批著名的画家，阎立本兄弟、大小尉迟、大小李将军、王维、吴道玄等等。他们活跃在唐代的历史舞台上，曾创作出许多杰出的绘画作品。但由先年代久远，加之自然的和人为的破坏，绝大多数作品都已经消失或残缺了。乾陵陪葬墓石刻线画因深埋于高等级的陪葬墓中而幸免于难，并且呈现出完整、清新的品相。更重要的是，乾陵陪葬墓石刻线画数量众多，内容丰富，水平高超。可以毫不夸张地说，它是唐代石刻艺术的杰作，是唐代绘画艺术的瑰宝，是唐人留给我们的重要文化遗产。

其次，它是我们认识唐代文化的重要资料。唐代是中国古代文化最为璀璨的时期之一，乾陵陪葬墓石刻线画作为唐代石刻艺术的瑰宝，在展现其艺术魅力的同时，也铺开了唐代社会生活的画卷，成为研究唐代历史不可多得的珍贵资料。石刻线画中侍女画居多，其服饰有短襦、披帛、长裙、云头履、线鞋、窄袖圆领长袍、大翻领长袍、条纹裤，发式有单螺髻、双螺髻、单刀髻、蝶形髻，头饰有各种钗、步摇、珠花，这些都是研究唐代文化最真实、最直接的资料。这些资料不仅使文献记载更具体直观，也弥补了文献记载的缺漏和不足。同时对研究唐代服饰、妆束的发展演变也有着积极意义。

石刻线画作为石椁的装饰，是身份的象征，是荣耀的体现，也更多地展示了宫廷生活，同时也反映了当时的丧葬制度，这些都为唐史研究提供了宝贵的资料。

再者，它有助于我们对唐代生态环境的认识。文献记载，唐人喜爱花鸟。乾陵石刻中的花草、树木种类繁多，林林总总。树木即有木槿、石枏、冬青、栀子之类。花卉则有郁金、百合、杜若、金盏与草菊等。鸟类有鸳鸯、告天子、绶带、青鸟、百灵子、伯劳、黄鹂、燕珩等十余种。昆虫中有蜻蜓、蝶、蜂等。花卉组合，层次分明，构图巧妙，纹饰布局，点面结合，不一而足。如在章怀太子墓椁内倚柱上刻的纹饰就有缠枝卷叶、缠枝海石榴、卷叶裹荷、卷叶海石榴、大叶海石榴等，其中以缠枝海石榴居多。除此之外，墓室庑殿门南窗棂上部刻有一对相向奔驰的翼马，以二株卷叶纹相间，中部直棱窗四周以草叶纹为饰，下部二猛虎相对而立，中间仍以草叶纹间隔，下部边缘则为卷叶纹。椁外象征性的殿门门楣上刻卷叶海石榴纹，一对舞凤尾部转化为海石榴叶，四周以海石榴纹装饰。永泰公主墓石门和石椁上这种线刻纹饰也广为分布，每一幅石刻线画周边都有纹饰镶边，使画幅相对独立，如石椁外壁东面的"直棱窗图"，上部以卷云纹为饰，接着是相向而舞的两凤，其尾部似也刻画为海石榴叶，中部窗棂四周以卷叶海石榴纹装饰，下部两雄狮相向而立，并以抱合式卷草图案相隔，底部饰卷叶纹。这些动物和植物，不仅表现了唐人的审美情趣，而且在一定程度上反映了唐代前期的生态环境。

石刻线画作为石刻艺术的一种，在民族文化的长河中举足轻重，在世界艺术史上独树一帜。有学者认为，"唐代石椁线刻是以绘画为标准，顺应石材特征，以刀代笔，以刻石代勾描而呈现其特有艺术风格。就刻石技法而言，唐代石椁线刻是由汉画像石中脱胎而出，汉代画像石采用凿刻方式，显然属于雕塑的技法表

现范畴。而石椁线刻的推刻勒石技法则与绘画中毛笔的行笔方式基本相同，具有明确的绘画属性，行刀方式、刀型变化及造型塑造都是追随绘画的转变而变化。其勒石技法的演变基本分为三个阶段：一为延续魏晋南北朝刻制技法的魏晋遗刀时期（630-689），二为模拟绘画线形的以刀拟绘时期（706-721），三为注重本体特性的抒发的以刀代笔时期（724—748）"[10]。乾陵陪葬墓石刻线画即处于第二阶段，在中国绘画史上具有承前启后的作用。宋元时期，石刻线画有式微的倾向，但仍出现过一些重要的作品。如宋代的《水陆斋戒仪神像图》，分三层刻绘天堂地府众神十八尊，无不具有修真度世之容。元代的《朝元仙仗图》、《玄宗问法图》，亦是高水平的宗教类石刻线画。明清时期，理学臻盛，表现孝行的石刻线画层出不穷。这些绘画在内容和技法上或多或少，都受到了唐代石刻线画的影响。由此可见，唐代石刻线画在中国绘画史上确实占有十分重要的地位。

Preface

Qianling Mausoleum is a mausoleum complex housing the remains of both Emperor Gaozong , the third emperor of the Tang Dynasty and his wife, China's first (and only) governing empress Wu Zetian. Featured by its grand and magnificence, Qianling Mausoleum is regarded as the NO. 1 Tang Dynasty Mausoleum on the Guanzhong Plain.

Although the underground palace of the main tomb of Gaozong and Wu Zetian is yet to be excavated, archaeologists have found, in the already unearthed attendant tombs of Prince Zhanghuai, Princess Yongtai and Prince Yide, many historical relics, among which are many exquisite line-engraved stone reliefs. Line-engravings are line-engraved representations on the stone. Since line-engraved art mainly uses lines to engrave figures on the stone, it is generally known as "line-engravings" or "stone-engravings" which represents a unique art style in China [1] apart from paper painting, mural painting, cliff painting and wood block. Viewed historically and realistically, the line-engravings unearthed in the attendant tombs of Qianling Mausoleum have outstanding artistic and historical values, which are the masterpieces of Tang dynasty stone engravings and attract historians' keen interest in discovering their fascination.

1

As the most important part of Tang dynasty line-engraving works, Qianling Mausoleum line-engravings have inherited and been greatly influenced by the line-engraving techniques of the earlier dynasties. Historical data shows that Chinese line-engraving art has a long history which can be dated back to the pre-Qin period. Archaeological discoveries showed that some pre-historic cliff paintings had adopted features of line-engraving art. On the stone coffins of the Shang and Zhou dynasties, the traces of line-engraving can also be observed.

During the Qin and Han dynasties, the first climax of stone-engraving in Chinese history, the main stone-engraving works were figure brick-engravings and figure stone-engravings, figures engraved in bricks and stones, with ghosts and human life as motifs, featured by shallow engraving. The Han dynasty figure stone-engraved unearthed at Songshan village, Jiaxiang county in Shandong Province is a typical representative of this period's achievements. The Songshan stone figure is divided into 4 parts, the part at the top describing the divine and spirits' world with Queen Mother of the West, immortals and demons as the major characters; the part at the bottom reflecting the earthly life of government officials; the two parts in between describing historical stories, among them are the story about the highly praised promise-keeping Prince Ji Qi of the State of Wu in the Spring and Autumn Period, and the story about the three righteous generals of the State of Qi of the same period, who committed suicide at court, for feeling ashamed of their misbehaviors and compromised virtues. Han dynasty line-engraved stone reliefs are found in brick-chambered tombs and cliff tombs[2].

The early Western Han dynasty (206 B.C.-A. D. 24)engraved stone coffins had doorways, trees

1. Wang Shucun, "A Brief Survey of Chinese Line-engraving", Chinese Fine Arts. Painting, vol.19, Shanghai People's Publishing House, 1998, p1.

2. Zhang Zijiang,"Stone Coffin Caskets Engravings during the Western and Eastern Han Dynasties", Identification and Appreciation of Cultural Relics, vol.8, 2011, p20.

and human figures as their main characters and enjoyed very a simple style. In the later Western Han dynasty, with more and more stone coffins being used, the contents of line-engraving grew richer, covering topics ranging from daily life of traveling, hunting, banqueting to legendary stories of Fu Xi, Nü Wa, Queen Mother of the West as well as immortals and ghosts. The Guolizhen stone coffin, now on display in Zoucheng Museum in Shandong Province, for example, has engraved figures of Thunder God, Rain God, Queen Mother of the West and other immortals on it.

Stone-engraving witnessed its prime in the Eastern Han dynasty (25-220 A.D.), which is attested by the many figure stone-engravings unearthed in Sichuan, Shandong, Henan, Shaanxi and Inner Mongolia, on which are figures of immortals and ghosts, people enjoying their daily life, historical stories as well as various decorating patterns, all having very high artistic value.

During the period of Wei, Jin, Southern and Northern dynasties, figure stone-engraving and brick-engraving began to decline but the wide spread of Buddhism greatly vitalized line-engraving with Buddhist figures as its main feature. Important Buddhist engravings usually have Buddha's life stories or Buddhist stories on them. One example is the stone engraving of the Northern Wei (475 A.D.) housed in Shaanxi History Museum, which is divided into 7 parts from the top to the bottom, telling in a serial stories of Buddha's life.

In the Sui and Tang dynasties line-engraving kept on its development and was mainly found in the religion-related areas and tombs. Religion-related line-engraving was motivated by the prosperous development of both Buddhism and Daoism during this period, while line-engraving in tombs became fully developed when engraved stone coffin caskets and gravestones became a trend.

Line-engravings in Tang tombs are mainly found on the lintels, leafs of the stone doors, the interior and exterior wall surfaces and columns of the stone coffins, a "stereotyped pattern" of the Tang funerary system as well as a general symbol[3]. According to archaeological data and practical observation, the main carrier of Tang tomb line-engravings are stone doors and stone coffin caskets , with the stones collected from the Jade Mirror Mountain in Fuping county of Shaanxi Province, tailored and polished as were needed.

Among the 17 attendant tombs of Qianling Mausoleum complex, five have been excavated, namely: the tomb of Prince Zhanghuai, tomb of Prince Yide, tomb of Princess Yongtai, tomb of Li Jinxing and tomb of Xue Yuanchao. Although line-engraved stone reliefs are found in all the five tombs, the authors of this book, however, have taken the line-engravings carved on the stone coffins of Prince Zhanghuai, Prince Yide and Princess Yongtai as their subject of study.

2

The tombs of Princes Zhanghuai, Yide and Princess Yongtai were all built during the years of 705-706 A. D. of Emperor Zhongzong's reign. Since the burial time of the three were close to each other, the size and funerary practices were very much similar. But owing to the differentiated positions and status of the three, the structures of the three tombs show some differences, which were reflected, in a way, by the line-engravings on their respective coffin.

Named Li Xian, Prince Zhanghuai was the second son of Emperor Gaozong and Empress Wu and was made crown prince on the third day of the sixth month of the second year of Shangyuan reign (675 A. D.) and was assigned to handle

3.Li Xingming, *Mural Paintings in Tang Tombs*, Shaanxi Fine Arts Publishing House, 2005, p138.

4.Liu Xu, Old Tang History, p1509.

5. Liu Xu, Old Tang History, p1480.

6. Ouyang Xiu New Tang History, p2026.

state affairs in the name of his Emperor father in the first year of Tiaolu Reign (679 A .D.), Prince Zhanghuai was the author of Important Records of the Court in 10 volumes[4], On the Vassal States in 30 volumes[5], and Important Records on Self-cultivation in 10 volumes[6]. He was the annotator of the History of the Later Han Dynasty.

In the first year of Yonglong Reign (680 A. D.) Li Xian was accused of treason, and was demoted to commoner rank. On the eighth day of the eleventh month of the first year of kaiyao Reign (681A.D.), he was exiled to Ba Prefecture (in modern Sichuan Province). On the 27th day of the second month of the first year of Wenming Reign(684 A.D.), Li Xian committed suicide in Ba Prefecture at the age of 31. Li Xian was honored a posthumous title of " Prince of Yong" by Empress Wu Zetian in the first year of Chuigong Reign (685 A.D.) and in the second year of Shenlong Reign (706 A.D), his remains were reburied near the tomb of Emperor Gaozong in Qianling Mausoleum complex.

Prince Zhanghuai's tomb is 180 meters long from north to south and 143 meters wide from east to west, covering an area of 25,740 square meters. The tumulus mound takes a trapezoidal shape and is around 18 meters high. In 1971 and 1972, archaeologists excavated Prince Zhanghuai's tomb and unearthed more than 600 pieces of relics. The stone coffin, 3.745 meters long, 2.85 meters wide and 1.85 meters high, was located at the rear tomb chamber. Consisting of 33 slates, the stone coffin has more than 40 elegant line-engravings carved on both the interior and exterior wall surfaces and columns.

Prince Yide, Li Chongrun, the eldest grandson of Emperor Gaozong and Empress Wu Zetian, as well as the the son of Emperor Zhongzong (Li Zhe)and his wife Empress Wei, was born in the second year of Kaiyao Reign (682 A.D.) and was created as Deputy Crown Prince by his grandfather Emperor Gaozong shortly after his birth. At the beginning of Wenming Reign (684 A.D.), after his father Emperor Zhongzong was deposed by Empress Wu Zetian, Li Chongrun

was reduced to commoner rank. In the first year of Shengli Reign (698 A.D.) when Li Zhe was restored as crown prince, Li Chongrun was renamed the Prince of Shao.

In the nineth month of the first year of Dazu Reign (701 A.D.), Li Chongrun offended his grandmother Empress Wu Zetian for discussing about Wu's lovers Zhang Yizhi and Zhang Changzong with his sister Li Xianhui, the Lady Yongtai and her husband Wu Yanji, and was caned to death at the age of 19. Li Chongrun was originally buried in the eastern capital of Luoyang. After Emperor Zhongzong was restored to the throne, he posthumously honored Li Chongrun as Crown Prince Yide and ordered that Li Chongrun be reburied with proper imperial honors, near the tomb of Emperor Gaozong in the Qianling Mausoleum complex in the second year of Shenlong Reign (706 A.D.)

Prince Yide's tomb is 256.5 meters in length and 214 meters in width, covering an area of 54,891 square meters. The grave mound takes a trapezoidal shape and is around 17.92 meters high. In the 1971 to1972 archaeological excavation, the stone coffin, 3.7 meters long, 2.82 meters wide and 1.87 meters high, was found at the rear tomb chamber, with 33 elegant line-engravings carved on both the interior and exterior wall surfaces and columns.

Li Xianhui, granddaughter of Emperor Gaozong and Empress Wu zetian, as well as daughter of Emperor Zhongzong and Empress Wei, was married to Wei Yanji, the Prince of Wei. In the first year of Dazu Reign (701 A.D.), at the age of 17, she secretly discussed with her brother Li Chongrun the issue of Empress Wu Zetian's lovers Zhang Yizhi and Zhang Changzong, and was forced to commit suicide. Li Xianhui was originally buried in Luoyang. After Emperor Zhongzong was restored to the throne in the first year of Shenlong Reign (705 A.D.), Li Xianhui was posthumously honored as Princess Yongtai and was reburied with honors. Her remains were interred, with her husband, at the Qianling Mausoleum complex.

From 1960 to 1964, archaeologists excavated the tomb of Princess Yongtai and unearthed numerous relics. Princess Yongtai's stone coffin is 3.77 meters long, 2.79 meters wide and around 2 meters high, with 33 elegant line-engravings carved on both the interior and exterior wall surfaces and columns.

The above-mentioned three stone coffins are all large in size, the line-engravings on the interior and exterior wall surfaces are 0.8 to 1.1 square meters in size. The interior and exterior columns are 0.44 square meters in size. On the wall surfaces are line-engravings of human figures (maidens and attendants), animals (birds and beasts), plants (flowers and vines) and objects (stones, buildings and utensils). On the columns, vines, branches, flowers, auspicious birds and beasts are engraved for decoration.

3

Reviewing the line-engravings in the attendant tombs in Qianling, we can clearly find that they mainly consist of figures and their actions. Taking those on the interior and exterior wall surfaces of the coffin casket of Prince Zhanghuai as an example, there are 14 line-engraving stone reliefs portraying 21 figures, all standing with different postures and expressions. As the funerary idea "serve the dead in the same way as they were alive" was observed at that time,

those stone-engravings chiefly display the life scenes of the ones buried in the tombs.

Counting from the west of the south interior wall surface of the stone coffin casket, we can see in the first line-engraving two maidservants. The left one wears a spiral-shaped hair bun with a beam hairpin, while the right wearing a hairpin in the shape of a phoenix. Both are in the same posture, standing straight with hands folded. There are three flowers, the middle being the gardenia, the other two looking like hibiscus rosa-sinensis flowers. On the lower right corner is rockery with a chickadee flapping above. The edge is ornamented with curly leaves.

In the second line-engraving, there are two maidservants, both standing on side elevation towards the same direction. The first wears a spiral-shaped hair bun, the second wearing two. They are dressed in the same type of costume, standing straight with hands folded. In the middle, there is a dahlia plant level with the eye, the leaves distributed in picturesque disorder. On its left is a horseradish plant, with two butterflies, and two birds, cuckoo and woodcock, fluttering above. The edge is ornamented with the interlocking camellia japonica design.

In the first line-engraving on the west wall surface, counting from the south, we can see a spindly maidservant, standing straight with hands folded. She wears a spiral-shaped hair bun,

Measurement of the Line-engravings on Princess Yongtai's Stone Coffin

Unit: cm

	Spec.	1st	2nd	3rd	4th	5th	6th	7th	8th	9th	10th
Interior Column	height	132	131.5	132.5	133.5	133	132.5				
	width	35	35.5	35.5	35.3	35.5	35				
Exterior Column	height	135	134.5	135	135	134	134	134	136	136	134
	width	35.5	35	35	35	35.5	35	33.5	33.5	35.5	34.5
Interior Wall Surface	height	131.5	134.5	135	130.5	132.5	130.5	130.5	135.5	130.5	136
	width	76.5	80	67.5	79	66	78	76	76	78	68.5
Exterior Wall Surface	height	136.5	137	136.5	136	136	136	136			
	width	76.5	80	68.5	80	66	77.5	76.5			
Remarks	Paintings are numbered from the northwest one in a clockwise direction.										

a shawl, a floor-sweeping gown and a pair of shoes with cloud pattern. On her left is a photinia serrulata-like plant, level with the eye. On her right is a pollia sorzogonensis steud, with two flying birds, pratincole and cuckoo, overhead. A dragonfly rests on the upper left corner. The edge is ornamented with large curly leaves, which are line-engraved with the underside scraped.

There are two maidservants in the second line-engraving. The left wears a spiral-shaped hair bun, pearl head-ornaments, a hairpin called *Buyao* (a hairpin adorned with movable flower branch-shaped pendants. It would constantly shake with the wearer's steps, hence the name "buyao", which means "shake as you walk". Most *buyaos* were made of gold, adorned with pearls and jade) and a pair of shoes with cloud pattern. She has graceful and comely complexion, standing straight with hands folded and seeming lost in thought. The right figure has on her head two spiral-shaped hair buns, wearing a round- neck flowery gown. A belt and a pouch tied at the waist, she is disguised as a man, a cloth bag in hand. A calendula plant in full blossom is in the middle, higher than the figures. On its left is a smartweed-like plant, level with the figures. On its right is an okra-like plant. Below is a Taihu Stone, a lily and two Chinese violets, a pair of bulbul birds flapping above the plant.

In the third one, there is a maidservant with two spiral-shaped hair buns, wearing pearl head-ornaments and a round-neck floor-sweeping gown and a pair of embroidered shoes, with a bonsai horseradish in hands. Bees and butterflies and dragonflies flutter above. Three siskins are flapping overhead. On the lower right corner is a beehive stone and a day-lily; a marigold is on the lower left corner.

In the first line-engraving on the north wall surface, there is a maidservant with slim and graceful figure, standing straight, deep in thought. She wears a spiral-shaped hair bun and a pair of embroidered shoes, having a pretty complexion, hands folded upon the bosom. This figure is carved with the head and feet reaching the top and bottom lines of the frame respectively, looking slim and tall. On her left is a camellia-like plant. An okra, whose stem growing straight upward and the leaves alternating, is on her right. On the upper left and right corners, are two woodcocks. The edge is ornamented with large curly leaves.

In the second line-engraving, there is a maidservant who wears a spiral-shaped hair bun, a shawl across her arms, a floor-sweeping gown and a pair of shoes with cloud pattern, standing straight with hands folded. On her left is a

Measurement of the Line-engravings on Prince Zhanghuai's Stone Coffin

Unit: cm

	Spec.	1st	2nd	3rd	4th	5th	6th	7th	8th	9th	10th	11th	12th	13th	14th
Interior Column	height	136	137	135	136	137	136								
	width	35	33	32	35	34	30								
Exterior Column	height	137	135	133.5	137	136	133	137	138	134	136	135	138	136	138
	width	36	34	34	34	33	33	34	30	35	33.5	35.5	34	31	36
Interior Wall Surface	height	126	128	131	130	130	125	125	125	124	124				
	width	80	75	69	81	68	79	83	74	67	73				
Exterior Wall Surface	height	131	130	132	131	132	127	128	132	130	133				
	width	81	75	67	80	63	74	81	74	68	69				
Remarks	Paintings are numbered from the northwest one in a clockwise direction.														

cheeseflower, level with the eye. Its stem grows straight upward, with two flower buds at the top. On her right is a day- lily with three . Above it a camellia is carved. A turtle-dove is flapping on the upper right corner. The edge is ornamented with large curly leaves, which are carved into convex leaves with the underside scraped.

In the first line-engraving on the east wall surface, a maidservant, with a flowerpot in hands, is collecting dew from the flowers. She wears a spiral-shaped hair bun, gazing at a blossoming flower. A shawl is thrown over her left shoulder, the drapery hanging straight downward. On her left is a lotus, and a forsythia is on the right. Below is websterite and grass. In the upper middle, there are two flapping yellowbirds with a butterfly flying in between. The edge is ornamented with curly pomegranate leaves.

A maidservant wears a phoenix crown, two hair buns with hairpins on both sides, a *Buyao*, a flowery blouse, a shawl, an ankle length gown, and embroidered shoes, standing straight with hands folded. Flowers and stones are carved as background ornaments. On her left is a shrub althea flower in blossom and a cowparsnip is on the right. Below is the rockery. Above the figure, two mandarin ducks fly on each side towards the same direction.

Carved in the first stone-engraving on the south exterior wall surface of the stone coffin are two maidservants. The first one on the right, in plump features, wears a spiral-shaped hair bun, a flowery blouse, a long shawl, and a floor-sweeping gown, standing with hands folded, looking demure in appearance. The one behind her also has a spiral-shaped hair bun on her head, disguised as a man. She wears robe of overturned collar, with a carved pot in hands, a belt and a sword at her waist. She is a head lower than the first figure, and seems to be an attendant. In the middle, there is a cotton rose in blossom. A bird, looks like turtle-dove, flying above on the left. The edge is decorated with broadleaf camellia japonica.

In the second one, there are two maidservants. The first one, slim and tall, wears a high butterfly-shaped hair bun, a shawl and a floor-sweeping gown, gazing at the flowers in supple and graceful carriage. She holds the fence with the left hand, the right one bending the branch. Behind her is a woman disguised as a man, a flower in hand. She wears an embroidered robe of overturned collar and a kerchief, smelling the flowers sideways, looking peaceful and relaxed. Below are a rock and three flowers. On her left is a magnolia flower in blossom, level with the figure. Behind the figures is a mallow with flowers and buds,

Measurement of the Line—engravings on Prince Yide's Stone Coffin

Unit: cm

	Spec.	1st	2nd	3rd	4th	5th	6th	7th	8th	9th	10th
Interior Column	height	133	134	134	133.5	133.5	134				
	width	34	34	34	33	34	34				
Exterior Column	height	135	134	134.5	134	134	135	134	134	134	135
	width	34	34	34.5	34.3	34.5	35	30.5	34	35	34
Interior Wall Surface	height	131	130.5	127.5	128	129	131	131.5	131	129	129
	width	80	79	68	74	68.5	80	80.5	66	72	68
Exterior Wall Surface	height	130	129	136.5	133.5	133.5	131.5	130			
	width	80.5	79	67	75.5	69.5	80	80			
Remarks	Paintings are numbered from the northwest one in a clockwise direction.										

carved in natural form, level with the magnolia flower. The edge is decorated with curly camellia japonica leaves.

The first one on the east wall surface depicts the south window bars of the hip-roofed palace hall. The pattern falls into three parts. In the upper part, two winged horses galloping from opposite directions, streaked with two curved leaves. The middle part is a ten-straight-bar window with adornment of grass and leaves around. The lower part, streaked with grass leaves across and curly leaves below, is occupied by two tigers with mouths wide open and paws stretched, as if ready to fight.

The second line-engraving symbolizes the doors of the palace hall with both architrave and lintel. Carved on the doors are curved camellia japonica leaves and a pair of phoenixes whose tails are converted into camellia japonica leaves, twigs in mouths. The four margins are figured with camellia japonica. The doors are decorated with 4 rows of 7 knurled rivets. In the middle of the doors, there is animal head applique holding rings. Two guards stand in front of the door. The left guard is a bowing eunuch with a broad face and a prominent cheekbone, holding a tablet representing his office. He wears a kerchief, two corners of which are hanging down covering his ears on both sides. The right one is a stout maidservant who wears a high hair bun, a shawl and a pair of shoes with cloud pattern, one arm hanging down, holding the shawl in hand, as if she was about to speak.

The third depicts the right window of the palace hall. The pattern is similar to that on the left one except that in the lower part there are two tiger-like animals. They both have a horn on head, seeming to be a pair of *xiezhi* (a fabulous animal reputed to be able to distinguish between good and evil).

In the first one on the north wall surface, a woman is disguised as a man, wearing a coronet of flowers and dressed in a round-neck robe. She stands at full face, holding a square cloth bag in hands. Above her are flapping birds and butterflies. On her left is a broadleaf hollyhock. On her right is an atractylodes, level approximately with the figure. Below is a Taihu Stone. The edge is decorated with broadleaf grass in a curved shape.

In the second line-engraving, two maidservants stand face to face. The left one wears two spiral-shaped hair buns, dressed in a round-neck gown, holding a painted pottery in hands. The right one wears a high spiral-shaped hair bun, a shawl, an ankle length gown, and a pair of shoes with cloud pattern, one hand up in the air and the other hanging down. There is a flower and a tree between the two figures. The flower looks like camellia whose leaves are like those of a holly, a thrush perching on it. Two birds, yellowbird and bluebird, are flapping on the upper right and left corners respectively. Four picked-flowers—a radix curcumae and a mallow on the right, a camellia and lily on the left—are carved on the four sides. Rocks are carved on the lower corner. The edge is decorated with large curly leaves.

It is obvious that, represented by the figure line-engravings in prince Zhanghuai's tomb, the line-engravings in the attendant tombs in Qianling Mausoleum show not only the eminent status of the ones buried in them but also the magnificence of the palaces. These line-engravings also display scenes of the brilliant court life and reflect the fashion and aesthetics of the upper-class court people. It is worth noting that animals and plants take up a large proportion in those line-engravings in the attendant tombs in Qianling Mausoleum. Objects such as dragon, phoenix, heavenly steed, unicorn, lion, camelbird, mandarin duck, crane, and some exotic animals and a variety of flowers and plants are depicted in

7. Li Jie, "Identification of Tang 'Line Drawings' ", Fine Arts Education, vol.1, 2011p7.

very conspicuous places. Although they merely function as the background ornaments in figure engraving, they integrate harmoniously with all sorts of figures, thus becoming an indispensable part of it.

4

The Tang figure line-engravings on the stone coffin caskets are an interpretive form of line-drawing.[7] The creators of line-engravings include the painters who framed the line-engraving manuscripts and the craftsmen who carved lines in the stones according to the manuscripts. The line-engravings in Qianling Mausoleum fall into two types according to their engraving techniques: line-engraving and line-engraving with the undersides scraped. Generally speaking, the line-engravings on the wall surfaces are mostly engraved in intaglio with thin lines using a graver. This kind of line-engraving embodies the features of line-drawings or iron-wire drawing. Line-engraving with the undersides scraped means to foreground the pattern by scraping off the stone surface skirting the external margins of the pattern, and then incise the outline with lines. The specific process of engraving is reflected by the engraved works on the west wall surface of the stone coffin of Prince Zhanghuai

As the west wall surface of the coffin usually sits very close to the west wall of the rear chamber, the line-engravings on it are relatively untidy and crude. Some are so near to the wall that it is hard to tell whether there are line-engravings on them. For example, the distance between the west wall of the stone coffin casket and the west wall of Princess Yongtai's tomb is only about 15-20cm. As dust lies thick in between and cannot be cleaned out, archaeologists cannot identify whether there are line-engravings on them. Between the west wall of the stone coffin and the

west wall of Prince Zhanghuai's tomb, though, there is a space of 50cm which allows a person to pass through. In general, the west walls of stone coffins casket were not meant for people to watch and therefore were engraved in haste, rough and simplified manner. Even the whiting used then for priming remains intact, leaving some original signs of doing the painting.

This offers evidence to the line-engraving techniques recorded in the Tang fiction Miscellaneous Morsels from Youyang, and is very valuable for studying the line-engraving art in the Tang dynasty. By comparing and observing the line-engravings in the Qianling tombs and in other tombs of the time, archaeologists figured out how these fine engraved decorations were made. First, the surface of slates or white marbles was polished, on which sample painting was drawn with a brush which had been dipped in the mixture of glue water and chalky clay. A rough draft was done by using the carving-knife to cut out very thin lines. Once the draft was finalized, the engraving was a non-stop work. Judging from the carving marks and the handwriting, some line-engravings were drafted and engraved by the same craftsman, others were drafted by one person and carved by another. As is recorded in Volume 5 of Miscellaneous Morsels from Youyang, "the exquisite engraved decorations in the Bodhi Temple in Pingkang Workshop is said to have been drafted by Zhen Fashi." Zhen Fashi is a master in mural painting in the Tang dynasty, enjoying equal popularity with Wu Daozi and Lu Lengqie. The fact of such famous painters drafting for line-engraving decorations shows that line-engraving art has attached great importance in the Tang dynasty.

Mr. Wang Shucun, a renowned scholar of art history, holds that before the Tang dynasty "line-engravings were mostly created by folk artisans"[8]. Though there is no clear record about

8. Wang Shucun, "The Development of Line-Engraving and It's Research Value", Fine Arts History Study, vol. 3, 2007, p68.

the engravers of the line-engravings in Qianling Mausoleum, archaeologists believe that they could not have been done by folk craftsmen. The reasons lie in two points: first, as princes or prince-sses, those buried in Qianling Mausoleum had very prominent social status; second, the contents of line-engravings show that the figures in the line-engravings were modeled on real people, the size of which is in accordance with their social status, which requires that painters be familiar with these people, to whom ordinary folk craftsmen could have no access. Therefore the drafts of these engravings were very likely be made by court painters and carving was done by first-class engravers. As a result, the line-engravings of this time have reached a very high artistic level.

The line-engravings in the attendant tombs of Qianling Mausoleum are vivid and lifelike, pleasing to the eye with soft and fluent cutting lines. One line-engraving carved on Prince Zhanghuai's stone coffin shows a beautiful maidservant who wears a bun shaped like a butterfly, a shawl and a floor-sweepins dress, her left hand holding the fence and her right hand posed in an attempt to pick flowering branch. With her body leaned to one side, she is gazing downward at the flowers in a very graceful posture. Another maiden, dressed up as a man, wears an embroidered robe with lapel, holds a flower in hand and leans her body to one side to smell the flowers in a leisurely poise.

In another drawing found on the interior wall surface of Princess Yongtai's coffin, a maidservant, wearing a spiral-shaped hair bun ornamented with a *Buyao*, is dressed in a short coat with its fronts tied into a knot in front of her chest and a floor-sweeping gown. She looks very graceful with thin and long eyebrows, a pair of pretty eyes and a tiny mouth. She holds the shawl up with two hands as if wanting to dance, which endows the still picture a sense of motion.

The dresses and adornments of the maidservants are varied, showing their own characteristics. Some maidservants wear single spiral-shaped bun, others wear double spiral-shaped buns; some wear knife-shaped bun and some wear kerchief. Some are dressed in short coat with shawls and a floor-sweeping gown. They wear high-heeled shoes decorated with cloud patterns. Still, there are some, who wear embroidered gown with lapels, striped trousers, woolen shoes, and leather belts with ornaments around the waists. In a line-engraving found on the stone gate of the east wall outside Prince Yide's tomb, two maidservants are dressed up by wearing phoenix crowns and court dresses, standing face to face with hands folded at the bosom, as if being on night guard for her master buried there. Plants and flowers are dotted around the maidens, and the door frame is decorated with curly leaf patterns. Two phoenixes flying towards each other on the door lintel. The whole picture is luxuriant and beautiful.

These line-engravings are all finely done, characterized by their fluency, vigorousness and liveliness. The engravers cut lines in a firm and steady manner, used strength evenly and made little change in the width of the lines. Therefore, the line-engravings are delicate and beautiful, fluent and smooth, and the artistic effect is created by using lines to form the shape and to bring out the charm of the pictures. As the contents of the pictures vary, the figures depicted are of different characters, some are gentle and lovely, some strong and powerful. As far as the composition of the pictures is concerned, different elements in the pictures are well arranged with regard to importance, harmony and unity, which shows the completeness as well as the neatness of the pictures, rendering the whole picture a sense of tidiness and a flavor of life without complexity.

Zhang Yanyuan of the Tang dynasty remarked

9. Chen Shouxiang, *History of Painting in the Sui and Tang Dynasties*, People's Fine Arts Publishing House, 2001.

in The Famous Paintings Through the Ages that "No painting can be done without using lines", which indicates the immense importance of lines to painting. According to some research, the painters in Tang dynasty developed in their own painting practice the traditional Chinese methods of depiction, such as "Wriggling Thread Depiction", "Iron Wire Depiction", which is expressive in showing something subtle, "Orchid Leaf Depiction", which is characterized by its variation, and contributed greatly to the depicting system of Chinese painting.[9] "Iron Wire Depiction" was originated during the era of Wei, Jin, Southern & Northern dynasties periods, which was mainly used to show the folds in dresses. The lines used in such a depicting technique are uniform in thickness, powerful and vigorous, and are shaped like folded iron wires, thus the name "Iron Wire Depiction". This depicting technique was developed greatly with "Emperors' Portraits Through the Ages" by Yan Liben as its representative work. In this masterpiece, the emperors' dresses and beards are depicted by using iron lines, making them vivid and lifelike.

"Iron Wire Depiction" was often used in the murals on the tomb walls in the Tang dynasty, especially in the line-engravings on the coffins. In the engravings on the wall surfaces of Princess Yongtai's coffin, each maidservant holds something in her hand, a silk fan, a jade plate, a dowry case, a dinner box or a candlestick. Gentle and refined, mild and charming, these figures are beautifully posed. Their dress belts are depicted mostly by using "iron wire lines", creating masterpieces of maiden line-engravings. "Orchid Leaf Depiction" is characterized by its variation of lines which are shaped like orchid leaves, as in the process of drawing the lines, force was used unevenly and the brush was removed from the paper or pressed on the paper alternatively, resulting in lines either thick or thin. It's said that such a depicting method was started by Wu Daozi, who often used such a method to portray figures and was praised for his excellent drawing skill in using the lines freely and boldly.

As an important part of paintings in Tang dynasty, the line-engravings in the attendant tombs of Qianling Mausoleum are mainly expressed by lines in a way that bears great resemblance to that used in line-drawing of traditional Chinese painting. But the line-engravings are based on plain and neat lines which are incised to form pictures. Line-engravings are carved on stones by using gravers to cut lines; therefore, they are paintings as well as sculptures. Only those who know painting art well and at the same time are skilled in sculpture are up to such tasks.

As is demonstrated by the line-engravings in the attendant tombs in Qianling Mausoleum, the painters at that time could express complicated contents by adopting lines expertly, while the engravers, on the other hand, could also show the width, weight, force, texture, ups and downs, rhythm and change of the lines in relation to the close connection between lines and shapes. Simple or complicated, lines are used according to the setting and meaning of the picture so that the whole picture is full of wit and is even more wonderful than the real ones in nature.

5

The line-engravings in the attendant tombs in Qianling Mausoleum are not only works of art, but also cultural relics with significant historical value. The authentic works by some famous painters and sculptors in the early Tang dynasty are preserved in them, offering us much valuable information about the of the Tang history and aclture.

First of all, they are important materials for studying paintings in Tang dynasty during which China's painting art flourished. Within 289 years, a large number of painters emerged, among them were Yan Liben and his brother, Yuchi senior and Yuchi junior, General Li senior and General Li junior, Wang Wei and Wu Daoxuan, to name a few of them. They were active in the fine arts arena and created numerous remarkable paintings. Due to natural disasters and human destruction, most paintings have got lost or damaged with age. The line-engravings in the attendant tombs in Qianling Mausoleum, being buried deep in the tombs of people with high social status, remain intact and complete. What is more important is that these line-engravings are large in number, rich in content and super in artistry. It's not exaggerating to say that they are masterpieces of line-engraving art, treasures of painting art in Tang dynasty, and important cultural relics left by the Tang people.

Secondly, these line-engravings are important documents, which help archaeologists know more about the cultures in the Tang dynasty, one of the most glorious periods in ancient Chinese history. As treasures, the line-engravings in the attendant tombs of Qianling Mausoleum, while displaying their artistic charm, present to us a spectacle of the social life in the Tang society and are rare materials for studying the Tang history. The figures in the line-engravings are mostly maidens, their clothes including short coats, shawls, long dresses, shoes decorated with cloud patterns, woolen shoes, long gowns with narrow sleeves and round collars, long robes with big lapels and striped trousers, their hairdos including single spiral-shaped bun, double spiral-shaped buns, knife-shaped bun, butterfly-shaped bun, and their headpieces including various hairpins and pearl head ornaments. All these are real and first-hand materials for the study of the Tang culture, which not only clarify the documentary records but also compensate for the records missing in the documents, and at the same time, facilitate the research into the development of the costumes in the Tang dynasty. Line-engravings as decorations on stone coffins serve as symbols of status and embodiment of glory. They reveal much about the court life and the contemporary burial system, providing valuable materials for studying the Tang history.

Third, they help archaeologists to learn about the ecological environment in the Tang dynasty. According to documents, the Tang dynasty people had great passion for flowers and birds. The flowers, grasses and plants found in line-engravings in the attendant tombs of Qianling Mausoleum are of various kinds. The trees include hibiscus, heathers, hollies, gardenias etc. The flowers include tulip, lily, pollia sorzogonensis steud, and calendula. The birds include mandarin duck, skylarks, terpsiphone paradise, blue bird, lark, butcherbird, yellowbird, oriental pratincole and so on. The insects include dragonfly, butterfly and bees. The flowers are well-arranged, and the pictures are ingeniously composed with the ornamental patterns expertly integrated. The ornamental patterns on the interior columns of the coffin casket of Prince Zhanghuai include twines and curly leaves, interlocking camellia japonica, curly lotus leaves, curly leaves and broadleaf camellia japonica, with interlocking camellia japonica being the most frequently adopted.

Besides, on the south window lattice of the door of the palace hall, two winged-horses galloping from opposite directions with two curly leaf patters in between are carved . The ten-straight-bar window was decorated with grass and leaves, below it are two vigorous tigers facing each other, streaked with grass and leaf patterns in between and curly leaves below. On the lintel of the symbolic door outside the coffin are carved curly camellia japonica, and a pair of phoenixes whose tails are converted into camellia japonica leaves.

The ornamental patterns are also widely used on the stone gates and stone coffin of Princess Yongtai's tomb. Surrounding each line-engraving are ornamental patterns, which help to frame each drawing. The ten-straight-bar windows on the east exterior wall surface is decorated with curly cloud patterns with two phoenixes above flying from opposite directions, their tails converted into camellia japonica leaves. The middle window lattice is decorated with curly

10. Li Jie, "The Art of Figure Line-engravings on the Tang Stone Coffins", Fine Arts, vol.11, 2011, p103.

camellia japonica leaves, two lions stand facing each other, separated by scroll designs and with curly leaf patterns below. These animals and plants not only show the aesthetic taste of people in the Tang dynasty, but also reflect the ecological environment in the early Tang dynasty.

As a unique type of stone-engraving, line-engraving has played a significant role in Chinese cultural history, as well as world art history. It is held by scholars that "The Tang line-engravings made use of the textures of stones and used knives to line-draw on the stone painting works, thus displaying its unique artistic flavor. Although Tang line-engraving art inherited the techniques of stone figure-engraving of the Han dynasty, which adopted chiseling, a technique in sculpturing, it is, nevertheless, different from sculpturing. The knife-carving methods share more resemblance with brush strokes in painting, so it bears the basic feature of painting, with the movements of knife and character depiction following those of painting. The engraving technique has experienced three periods. The first period was the further development of Wei, Jin, Southern and Northern dynasties' methods, known as "inherited Wei and Jin cutting techniques" (630-689 A.D.). The second period was a time when engravers imitated brush painting techniques, which is regarded as "knife imitating brush"period (706 -720 A.D.). The third period stressed on a natural expression by knife itself, thus known as "painting with knives"period (724-748 A.D.)[10].

Line-engravings in the attendant tombs of Qianling Mausoleum belong to the works of the second period, thus, serving as a link between the previous period and following period. During the Song and Yuan dynasties, line-engraving showed a declining trend in general, but important works did emerged in this period, among them were the Song dynasty line-engraving *Divines from the Shilu Studio* which depicted, in three parts, 18

divines in the heaven and the hell, each with a facial expression of self-cultivation and saving all sentient beings.

The Yuan dynasty produced two important line-engravings, The Eighty-seven Immortals and Emperor Xuanzong Inquiring Dharma, both were religion-related line-engravings with first-class quality. During the Ming and Qing dynasties, the booming of Neo-Confucianism brought about many line-engravings with filial piety as their motif. Both the contents and techniques of Ming and Qing line-engravings were more or less influenced by the Tang line-engravings, which attests to the fact that Tang line-engravings play an important role in Chinese fine arts history.

まえがき

　　乾陵は唐高宗李治と女皇帝武則天の合葬墓であり、非常に雄大で、「関中唐陵の冠」と称賛されている。目下のところ、乾陵の地宮は発掘をしていないが、考古学者によって陪葬墓の章懐太子墓、永泰公主墓、懿徳太子墓より大量の文物が発掘されている。その中には多くの精美な石刻線画が含まれている。石刻線画とは、鐫刻技法を用いて石板に絵画を彫刻した作品である。一般的に、石板の上に絵を線刻するものであるから、線刻画或いは石刻画と称される。その作品は紙・壁・岩・木板に描かれる絵画とは異なり、「我が国の芸術界における特有な芸術」と称されている[1]。歴史学と実物の観察から考えて見ると、乾陵陪葬墓から出土した石刻線画の芸術的な価値と史料的な価値は極めて高く、永遠の魅力を備えた唐朝石刻芸術の傑作であり、研究をより一層進める価値があると考える。

一

　　乾陵陪葬墓の石刻線画は唐代石刻線画の重要な構成部分である。唐代石刻線画は前代の石刻線画を基礎として発展してきたものであるので、前代の石刻線画の影響を一定程度受けている。

　　ある資料によると、中国石刻線画の歴史は非常に長く、先秦時代にまで遡ることができる。考古学者が発見した先史時代の岩画には、石刻線画の特徴を見出すことができる。商周時期の石棺、石槨には既に石刻線画の痕跡が発見された。秦漢時期は中国石刻線画史上、第一のピークである。この時期の石刻線画は、主に浅く彫刻する画像磚、画像石であり、鬼神の世界と人間の生活を描いたものである。１９８０年、山東省嘉祥宋山村で出土した画像石はその典型的な事例である。この画像石は四層あり、上層は西王母、仙人、精霊を描く鬼神世界、下層は官吏等の人物を描いて現実世界を表現したものであり、中間両層に描かれるのは「季杞挂剣

（季杞剣を掛ける）」、「二桃殺三士（二桃もて三士を殺す）」などの歴史故事である。一般的に、漢代の画像石棺は磚室墓或いは崖墓によく見られる[2]。前漢早期の画像石棺は、主に門闕・樹木・人物など比較的簡単な内容が描かれていた。前漢晩期になると、石棺墓が増加して、線刻画の内容も豊富になっていった。現実生活を描いた出行・狩猟・舞踊の様子の他に、伏羲・女媧・西王母などの伝説上の人物や、鬼神の姿も描かれるようになった。山東省鄒城県博物館が所蔵する郭里鎮に出土した石槨には雷公・雨師（雨乞い師）・西王母が彫刻されている。その後の後漢時代は、画像石の全盛期であった。考古学者は四川・山東・河南・陝西・内モンゴルなどの地域で大量の画像石を発見した。その内容は鬼神の姿や庶民の生活、歴史の物語、装飾模様などに及んでおり、比較的高い芸術レベルに達している。

　　魏晋南北朝時代、仏教の発展は石刻線画に新たな活力を与えた。この時期、画像磚・画像石は衰退するが、仏教造像の製作が流行し日に日

[1] 王樹村（1988）「中国石刻線画略史」『中国美術全集・絵画編』19，上海人民出版社，p.1
[2] 張孜江（2011）「漢時期的画像石棺石芸術」『文物鑑定与鑑賞』8，p.20
[3] 李星明（2005）『唐代墓室壁画研究』陝西人民美術出版社，p.138

に勢いを増していった。重要な仏像には往々として、仏陀の出生譚、仏教伝来や仏教の故事が彫刻される。例えば、陝西省歴史博物館が所蔵する北魏皇興五年（４７１）造像は、七層に分かれており、上から連環画形式で仏陀の伝記が描かれている。隋唐時代になると、石刻線画はそのまま発展して、ますます盛んとなった。この時期、石刻線画は二つの領域で盛んになる。一つは宗教世界であり、もうひとつは陵墓の中である。前者は魏晋南北朝期の余慶を受け、引き続き仏教道教の繁栄下で発展した。大雁塔の門楣に刻まれている「説法図」と天尊像の台座に刻まれた道士供養図は、宗教的石刻線画の代表である。後者は石槨墓葬と墓誌碑刻の流行によって繁栄した。

　　唐代墓葬の中の石刻線画は主に石門の門楣・門扇と、棺槨の内側・外側に刻まれる。ある学者は、これが唐代墓葬線刻画の「固定的形式」であり、普遍的でシンボリックな意味があると考えている[3]。考古資料と実物の観察から考えると、乾陵陪葬墓における石刻線画は石門と石槨の形態を取っている。その石材は陝西省富平県玉鏡山より採石されたと思われ、すべて丁寧に磨かれて加工処理がされており、石材の大きさは石門と石槨の実際の必要に応じて決められた。線刻画は石門の門楣・門扇、石槨の内外の倚柱と廂板の上に刻まれる。乾陵には少なくとも１７の陪葬墓が存在し、すでに章懐太子墓、懿徳太子墓、永泰公主墓、李瑾行墓、薛元超墓の五基が発掘されている。考古学者はそれらの墓葬の中から、少なからぬ石刻線画を発見した。本稿では章懐太子墓・永泰公主墓・懿徳太子墓の石槨の石刻線画についてのみ、整理を行いたい。

二

　　章懐太子墓・永泰公主墓・懿徳太子墓は、唐中宗神竜元年（７０５）から神竜二年にかけて造営された。埋葬時期は大体同じであるので、墓葬の制度と規模も似ている。しかしながら、その三人は身分、地位も異なるので、墓葬形態にも差異が存在する。そのような差異は石棺の石刻線画にも反映されている。

章懐太子墓の石槨における石刻線画のサイズ統計表
単位：センチメートル

	規格	第一枚	第二枚	第三枚	第四枚	第五枚	第六枚	第七枚	第八枚	第九枚	第十枚	第十一枚	第十二枚	第十三枚	第十四枚
内柱	高さ	136	137	135	136	137	136								
	幅	35	33	32	35	34	30								
外柱	高さ	137	135	133.5	137	136	133	137	138	131	136	135	138	136	138
	幅	36	34	31	34	33	33	31	30	35	33.5	35.5	31	31	36
内壁	高さ	126	128	131	130	130	125	125	125	121	124				
	幅	80	75	69	81	68	79	83	74	67	73				
外壁	高さ	131	130	132	131	132	127	128	132	130	133				
	幅	81	75	67	80	63	71	81	74	68	69				
備注	順序は西北から時計回り														

[1] 「藝文志三」「新唐書」59、p.1509
[2] 「藝文志二」「新唐書」58、p.1480
[3] 「経籍志下」「旧唐書」47、p.2026

　　章懐太子李賢は高宗李治と武則天の第二子であり、上元二年（６７５）六月三日、太子に立てられた。儀鳳四年（調露元年、６７９）に勅命を奉じて監国となった。『春宮要録』十巻[4]、『列藩正論』三十巻[5]、『修身要録』十巻[6]を撰し、また『後漢書』に注釈を加えた。永隆元年（６８０）「謀逆」の罪で廃位された。開耀元年（６８１）十一月八日、巴州に流され軟禁された。文明元年二月二十七日、巴州の邸宅で自殺を命じられた。享年わずか３１歳である。垂拱元年（６８５）に武則天により「雍王」を追封され、神竜二年（７０６）に乾陵に遷葬された。墓園は南北１８０メートル、東西１４３メートル、面積は２５７４０平方メートル。封土は覆斗形で、約１８メートルある。１９７１年から１９７２年にかけて、考古学者はその墓を発掘し、文物約６００件を発見した。石椁は墓室後室にあり、３３の石板からなり、全長3.745メートル、奥行き2.85メートル、高さ1.85メートルである。石椁内外に４０幅の線刻画が描かれている。

　　懿徳太子李重潤は唐高宗と武則天の嫡孫であり、唐中宗と韋皇后の長男である。開耀二年、東宮内殿にて生まれた。永淳元年（６８２）皇太孫となったが、文明元年（６８４）中宗が廃位

されたため、庶民になった。６９８年、中宗が再び皇太子となると、邵王に封ぜられた。大足元年（７０１）九月、永泰公主とその婿の魏王武延基とともに張易之兄弟が後宮に出入りしていることを議論したので、張易之の讒言を受けた。武則天は中宗に厳重な捜査を命じ、その結果杖殺された。享年わずか１９歳、洛陽に埋葬された。中宗復位後に懿徳太子を追封され、神竜二年（７０６）に帝王の礼を以て改めて乾陵に陪葬された。その墓園は縦２５６.５メートル、横２１４メートル、面積５４８９１平方メートルで、封土は覆斗形である。１９７１から１９７２年にかけて発掘調査がなされ、墓室後室より大型の石椁が発見された。石椁は全長3.7メートル、奥行き2.82メートル、高さ1.87メートルである。石椁の内外の倚柱及び椁壁上には精美な線刻画が合計33幅も描かれている。

　　永泰公主は唐高宗と武則天の孫にして、中宗と韋皇后の娘である。久視元年（７００）永泰郡主に封ぜられ、食邑一千戸を食み、魏王武延基に嫁いだ。大足元年（７０１）、張易之入宮事件を議論したので、自殺を命じられた。享年わずか１７歳、洛陽に埋葬された。神竜元年、永泰公主に追封され、有司の手により礼式を備えて改

懿徳太子墓の石椁における石刻線画のサイズ統計表
単位：センチメートル

	規格	第一枚	第二枚	第三枚	第四枚	第五枚	第六枚	第七枚	第八枚	第九枚	第十枚
内柱	高さ	133	134	134	133.5	133.5	134				
	幅	34	34	34	33	34	34				
外柱	高さ	135	134	134.5	134	134	135	134	134	134	136
	幅	34	34	34.5	34.3	34.5	35	30.5	34	35	34
内壁	高さ	131	130.5	127.5	128	129	131	131.5	131	129	129
	幅	80	79	68	74	68.5	80	80.5	66	72	68
外壁	高さ	130	129	136.5	133.5	133.5	131.5	136			
	幅	80.5	79	67	75.5	69.5	80	76.5			
備注	順序は西北から時計回り										

葬され、翌年、改めて乾陵に夫の武延基とともに陪葬された。1960年から1964年にかけて、考古学者はその墓に対して科学的な発掘を行い、大量の文物を発見した。その石槨は全長3.77メートル、奥行き2.79メートル、高さは約2メートル、石槨の内部・外部の柱及び壁面に精美な線刻画が合計33幅刻まれている。

上述の三基の倍葬墓の石槨は規模が比較的大きく、内壁・外壁の石刻線画の面積は0.8～1.1平方メートル、内外柱の面積は0.44平方メートル前後である。廂板には、主に人物（仕女・僕従）、動物（飛鳥・獣）、植物（花・蔓草）と無生物（石頭・建築・器物等）を描く。これが石刻線画の主体である。倚柱には蔓草・折枝・花卉・祥鳥・瑞獣などが描かれており、これらは装飾の役割を果たしている。

三

乾陵陪葬墓石刻線画の考察から、我々は人物とその活動が主な主題であることを明確に見てとることができる。ここでは章懐太子墓石槨内外壁の石刻線画を例として考察を進める。章懐太子墓石刻の人物画は14幅あり、21人の人物が線刻される。画中の人物は全て立ち姿であり、表情と姿勢はそれぞれ異なっている。当時、「死を視ること生のごとし」という葬送理念が励行されていた。石刻線画は墓主の生前の生活の様子を表している。

石槨の内側南壁の線刻画を西から東に順次にかぞえて行くと、第一幅目には侍女が二人描かれている。左側の侍女は螺髻をして、簪をさしている。右側は鳳凰を象った簪をさしている。二人ともに手を合わせた姿勢で立っている。線刻される花は三本、中央はクチナシ、左右両側は扶桑である。右下には拳石がある。上部には一羽のシジュウカラ（山雀）が飛んでいる。絵の縁は蔓草（巻葉）で飾られている。第二幅は侍女が同じ方向に向かって斜めに立っている。前方の侍女の髪型は単螺髻であり、後方は双螺髻である。二人の服装は同じで、ともに手を合わせて立っている。中央部にはダリア（大理菊）が一株、目線の高さまであり、枝葉がよく広がっている。左は山葵一株、その上部を二羽の蝶が飛んでいる。さらに鳥が二羽、一羽はカッコウ（杜鵑）であり、もう一羽はウッドコック（山鷸）である。縁飾りには椿（海石榴）の飾りがついている。

永泰公主墓の石槨における石刻線画のサイズ統計表
単位：センチメートル

	規格	第一枚	第二枚	第三枚	第四枚	第五枚	第六枚	第七枚	第八枚	第九枚	第十枚
内柱	高さ	132	131.5	132.5	133.5	133	132.5				
	幅	35	35.5	35.5	35.3	35.5	35				
外柱	高さ	135	134.5	135	135	134	134	134	136	136	134
	幅	35.5	35	35	35	35.5	35	33.5	33.5	35.5	34.5
内壁	高さ	131.5	134.5	135	130.5	132.5	130.5	130.5	135.5	130.5	136
	幅	73.5	80	67.5	79	66	78	76	76	78	68.5
外壁	高さ	136.5	137	136.5	136	136	136	136			
	幅	76.5	80	68.5	80	66	77.5	76.5			
備注	1.幅目は石槨の西北の位置にあり、そこから時計回りに描かれている。順を追って見て 2.線刻画の順序は西北から時計回りで、第1幅は石槨の西壁北側の1枚目にあたると推定（以下の表も同様）。										

西壁の線刻画は南から北側に向かって描かれ、第一幅は、痩せた侍女が一人手を合わせて立っている。侍女は螺髻し、肩掛けを羽織って、ロングスカートを地面にひきずり、雲頭鞋を履いている。その左側にヘザー（石柑花）が一輪、それは侍女の目のあたりの高さである。右には杜若（カキツバタ）一輪、上部には飛鳥が二羽、一羽はツバメで、もう一羽は杜鵑である。左上には蜻蛉が飛んでいる。縁飾りは大巻葉で額縁の線にまで係って線刻されている。第二幅は侍女二人、左の侍女の髪型は螺髻で、花の形をした簪と歩揺を差し、雲頭鞋を履いている。侍女は艶やかで、両手を合わせて立っていて、何か考え事をしているようである。右の侍女は双髻をして、丸襟の花模様の衣装を着ている。腰に帯を巻き巾着を付けて男装しており、手には風呂敷包みを捧げ持っている。中央部には金盏菊類（マリーゴールド）一輪、その丈は侍女の身長と同じである。右には葦一つ、人と同じ高さである。下には太湖石一つ、上に百合一輪と菫二輪が描かれている。上部には、ヒヨドリのつがいが大空に羽ばたいている。第三幅は双髻を結った侍女で、花形の簪をさし、丸襟の服にロングスカートを身に着け、刺繍の靴を履いている。ワサビの植木を両手で持っている。彼女の上部には蜂や蝶・蜻蛉が舞っている。雀が三羽、空を飛んでいる。右下に窠石が一塊、スイカズラ黄花（金針花）が一本、左にはマリーゴールドが一株生えている。

北壁の第一幅目には一人の侍女が描かれている。侍女は直立して考え事をめぐらしている。螺髻を結い、端麗な顔立ちで足取りは軽やか、両手を胸の前で組んでおり、頭と足は絵の縁取りに接するほど身長が高い。その左側は茶花一輪、右側に一輪の山葵が高くて茂っている。上部両側にはヤマシギ一対がある。縁飾りは大きな巻葉模様である。第二幅目もまた侍女が一人、螺髻を結い、手を胸の前で合わせて立っており、肩掛けを腕に羽織り、長い袖を地面に引き摺り、雲頭鞋を履いている。左にはマロー一本、人の目線の高さまで真っ直ぐ生えており、その頂部

には花が二房咲いている。右側はニッコウキスゲが一株、花には三つの蕾がついている。その上部には、椿が刻まれている。右側上部には一匹の鳩が飛翔する。縁飾りは大巻葉で、縁取りの線に葉がかかっている。

東壁第一幅は、一人の螺髻の侍女一人描かれる。両手には鉢を持ち、花についた露をとっているような姿である。肩掛けは左肩にかけ、服の模様は真っ直ぐ下を向いている。左には蓮一本、右には連翹一本。下はバン石と小草がある。上部中間は蝶、両側はマヒワが一羽ずつ飛んでいる。縁飾りには巻葉の石榴をもって縁を飾っている。さらに侍女が一人、頭に鳳凰模様の冠を戴き、双髻に簪を斜めにさしている。花柄の服に肩掛けと長衣を纏い、刺繍の靴を履いて、両手を合わせて立っている。背景は花や石で、左側にはハイビスカス一輪、右側はアンジェリカ、下には拳石がある。人物の上部両側に鴛鴦二羽が同じ方向に向かって飛んでいる。

石椁の外側南壁の第一幅には侍女が二人描かれている。右前は螺髻を結い、顔はふっくらしている。花柄の服に長肩掛けにロングスカートを穿き、手を合わせて斜めに立ち、きちんとしたおもむきである。後方の螺髻を結った侍女は男装している。折り襟の長衣を着て、両手に花模様の鉢を持っている。腰に帯を締めて、刀を差している。身長は前方の侍女の肩ぐらいで、侍従のようである。真中に芙蓉一本、花が咲いている。左上に鳥一羽、鳩のようである。縁飾りに葉の大きな椿がついている。第二幅目は女中二人。前の人は高い蝶髻をし、肩掛けをかけ、ロングスカートを穿いている。腰をかがめて花を見つめている。左手は欄干にかけ、右手は花を折っている。身体はすんなりしていて、姿態がしなやかで美しい。後ろの人は男装し、刺繍の折り襟の長衣を着て、帽子を被っている。手に花を持ち、かがんで花を嗅いでいる姿はのんびりしている。下には大きな石と花が三本ある。左側の辛夷は人の高さで花が咲いている。人物の後ろにはマローが一輪、高さは辛夷と同じで、花のほか蕾もあり、自然な姿である。

縁飾りの巻葉には椿がついている。

東側第一幅は廡殿門の南窓格子として描かれる。絵画は三つ部分で構成される。上段は翼馬（ペガサス）が二匹、向き合って疾走している。二匹の中間には巻葉模様が施されている。中段は10本の窓格子で、周囲は草葉模様である。下段は二匹の猛虎である。二匹は互いに向かって立ち、牙をむき爪を振り上げ、今にも相手に飛びかかろうとしている。二匹の中間を草葉紋様で隔て、下辺は巻葉紋様である。

第二幅目は御殿の門をかたどっている。門には枋額と門楣がついている。上部に刻まれた一対の鳳凰は花をくわえて舞っている。その尾は椿の葉に変わって縁飾りの椿模様と一体になっている。門は二つの扉からなり、門扉には横一直線四列、一列ごとに七本、花泡釘の模様が施されている。門扉の中央部にノッカーがついている。門の前には門衛が二人いる。左は宦官で、右は侍女である。宦官は四角い顔で、頬骨が突き出ている。腰をかがめて笏を持ち、頭巾をかぶり、その両端は長く垂れて、耳を覆い隠している。侍女はふっくらしていて、髷を高く結んでいる。肩掛けをかけ、雲頭鞋を履いている。片腕は垂れて肩掛けを手に持ち、何か話そうとしているようである。三幅目は御殿の門の右窓である。紋様は左窓と同じである。ただし下部には虎のよう獣が二匹向かい合っている。その容貌は角が生えた神獣獬豸のようである。

北壁第一幅目には男装した一人の女性が描かれている。女は花の冠をかぶり、丸襟の長衣を着、正面に向かって両手に四角い風呂敷包みを持っている。上部に鳥や蝶がある。左側は広葉タチアオイである。右はオケラ一本、人と同じぐらいの高さがある。下には太湖石があり、周りに大きい巻葉模様がついている。第二幅目には、二人の侍女が向かい合わせで立っている。左は双螺髻を結い、丸襟の長衣を着、手に色彩上絵を施した鉢を持っている。右は高螺髻を高く結び、片手を高く持ち、一方の手は垂らしている。肩掛けにロングスカート、雲頭鞋を履いてい

る。両者の中間には花と木が一つずつある。花は椿に似ているが、葉はモチノキに似ている。木には画眉鳥が止まっている。上部に鳥が二匹飛んでいる。左はコウライウグイスで、右は青鳥である。その周囲には花が4本ある。右はチューリップとゼニアオイで、左は椿と百合である。下部は山石が描かれており、周囲の縁飾りには巻葉紋様が施されている。

言うまでもなく、章懐太子墓人物画に代表される乾陵陪葬墓石刻線画は、墓主の高い身分と生前住んでいた宮殿の華麗さを表現したものであり、当時の宮廷生活の情景、上層社会の流行と美意識が反映されている。もう一つ注目に値するのは、乾陵陪葬墓石刻線画の題材として植物と動物が、高い比重を占めていることである。飛龍・鳳凰・翼馬（ペガサス）・麒麟・獅子・駝鳥・鴛鴦・鶴、そのほかの珍獣と草花もかなり目立っている。それらは装飾や人物を引き立てるのが主な役割とは言え、画面中の姿態は様々な人物と調和し、画面全体で不可欠な要素となっているのである。

四

唐代の石槨人物線画は、言うなれば「白描」を翻訳するような手法を取っている[7]。まず、石線画の製作者は二つに分けることができる。線画を下書きする創作者と下書きに基づいて線画を刻する職人である。乾陵陪葬墓石刻線画の彫刻法には、おおむね二つの形式が存在する。「線刻」と「減地線刻」である。おおむね言えば、廡板の石刻線画の多くは、細い線をもって陰刻する手法を採用している。直接、刀を用いて線と模様を陰刻するのである。この種の線刻は、「白描」あるいは「鉄線描」の特徴を備えている。「減地線刻」は「剔底線刻」ともいう。すなわち、花紋の輪郭に沿って石面の表層を削り取り、花紋の部分を浮かび上がらせ、然る後に再び輪郭の内側の線を陰刻するのである。その手法を用いた具体的な事例として章懐太子墓石槨の西壁

が挙げられ、その製作手順を窺い知ることができる。一般的に石椁の西壁は墓室後室の西壁に接するので、その線刻は粗雑に刻まれることが多い。時には西壁に密接するので、石刻線画があるかどうかさえ判断しにくい場合もある。例えば、永泰公主石椁の西壁はその一例である。石椁西壁と墓室西壁との間はわずか15センチ~20センチしかない。土を取り除くことができないので石椁外側の西壁は石刻線画の有無も知ることができない。ただし、章懐太子墓の場合は石椁西壁と墓室西壁との間は50センチぐらいで、人一人通れる距離がある。総じていえば、椁外西壁はもともと観賞用ではないので、彫刻も簡単でいい加減である。チョークなど製作当時の痕跡もいくつか残っている。このような事実は『酉陽雑俎』の中の線刻方法に関する記載を裏付ける。石椁の線刻画は、唐代石刻芸術の重要な研究資料なのである。章懐太子墓石椁と同時期の他の墓中の石刻線刻画を比較してみると、我々は線刻画の製作過程を知ることができる。まず、青石と漢白玉の表面をきれいに磨き、軽膠とチョークを混ぜたものを毛筆につけ、石に下書きを描く。描かれた下書きに沿って、彫刻刀で極めて細い線を刻み下図を確定する。そのあと、もう一度彫刻をして線刻画を完成させる。刀痕と筆跡から判断して、一人で二つの工程をやり遂げる部分と、一人が原画を描き、もう一人が彫刻をする部分があることが分かった。『酉陽雑俎』巻五には「平康坊菩提寺の中を飾る彫刻は新奇で優れており、鄭法士の手によると伝わっている。」という記載がある。鄭法士は唐代の壁画の名人で、呉道子、盧楞伽と同様に有名である。彼らが石刻の原稿を担当するのであるから、唐代では線刻がかなり重要視された芸術形式であったことがわかる。

著名な美術史家王樹村は「石刻線画の作品

は、民間職人の手によるものが多い」と言っている[8]。乾陵陪葬墓石刻線画の作者は誰であるか、文献には明確な記載はない。ただ明らかなのは乾陵陪葬墓の墓主は親王であれ、公主であれ、特殊な身分の人だということである。線刻画の内容から見れば、画中の人物の姿は実生活を反映していることが多い。彼女たちの身長と太り具合も身分と地位に関係している。石刻線画の作者は恐らく墓主の生活をよく知っている人物なのであろう。これは一般人のよくするところではない。故に、線刻画の下図は宮廷画師の手になる可能性がきわめて高い。彫刻担当の職人もおそらく彫刻の名手であろう。石刻線画そのものから見ても、確かに乾陵陪葬墓の線刻画はかなりの高水準に達している。

乾陵陪葬墓の石刻線画の造形は生き生きしており、線や紋様の筆致は流麗で柔らかく、非常に美しい。例えば、章懐太子墓石椁石刻線画の中には、一人の侍女が蝶形の高い髻を結い、身には肩掛けを覆い、ロングスカートを地面に引き摺り、左手は竿を支え、右手は枝を折るような姿をしている。なお、体を斜めにして高い所から花を見下ろし、体つきはたおやかである。もう一人の侍女は男装をして、襟の開いた刺繍入りの長衣を着て一輪の花を持ち、その香りを俯いて嗅ぐような、ゆったりとした様子である。

また、永泰公主墓石椁の北側内壁には、「披巾侍女図」がある。そこには、螺髻を結い簪を揺らしながら歩く侍女が描かれている。その侍女は丈の短い上着を肩に羽織って臂をあらわにし、両襟を胸の前で結び、ロングスカートを穿いて裾を地面にひきずって歩いている。柳のように細い眉に鳳凰のようにクリッとした瞳、サクランボのような小さな口、まるでほっそりとした少女のようである。その侍女は肩掛けを両手で載せ、ひらひらと舞うように見える画面は静止し

[7] 李傑（2011）「唐「白描」辨」『藝術教育』1。
[8] 王樹村（2007）「石刻線画之発展及其研究価値」『美術史研究』3、p.68。

ているが、非常に躍動感がある。その他の侍女の服飾も特徴がある。ある者は単螺髻を結った頭を梳き、またある者は双螺髻を梳く人もいる。そして、単刀髻を梳いて頭巾を被っている者もいる。あるいは短い上着に肩掛けを羽織って、ロングスカートを引き摺り、雲頭飾りの靴を履く者や、折り襟の長衣にストライプのズボンを履き、革製のベルトを腰にしめている者もいる。彼女たちはすべて装飾品を身に着けている。

　もう一つの例は、懿徳太子墓石槨の外東壁の石門の石刻線画である。そこには、侍女二人が描かれている。彼女たち派手に着飾り、頭には鳳凰形の冠を戴き、宮服を身に着け、手を合わせて向かい合って立っている。まるで墓の主人のために宿直をするようである。侍女の周りにも植物と花卉の飾りがあり、石門框の周囲は巻葉紋で飾られている。門楣には向かい合う2匹の鳳凰が描かれており、画面全体から非常に華麗な印象を受ける。これらの石刻線画はすべて細緻を極めており、なめらかで、力強く、そうした特徴がはっきりとしている。職人は線刻をする時の筆致は穏やかで、力を均等に制御しているので、線の太さの変化も小さく、秀でており流麗で闊達である。線を以て造型し、形は線によって生じ、線によって神髄を表すという芸術的効果に達している。

　画面の内容から見ると、描写した人物の性格は、糸のように柔らかなものもあれば、鉄のように力強いものもあり、1つにとどまらない。構図から見ても、内容の軽重によって主要なものと副次的なものを明確に区別して、画面の調和と整斉画一を原則として内容を定めており、構図が定められているので、完成された画面だけでなく整った図案を際立たせるのである。画面全体をして明晰かつ厳格な生活の息吹に富ませるだけでなく、簡明で全く無駄な所がない。

唐の張彦遠は『歴代名画記』の中で「無線者非画也（線無きは画に非ず）。」と言っている。これよって線が絵画にとってどんなに重要かが分かる。研究によれば唐代の画家はペンを使っており、その過程で中国の伝統的な「高古游糸描」が発展した。それに、含蓄のある表現を得意とする「鉄線描」、または起伏の変化に優れる「蘭葉描」は、すべて中国画筆法の「描法」体系に不朽の貢献を果たした。[9]「鉄線描」は魏晋南北朝の時にすでに存在していた。この描き方は主に服装や持ち物のしわの紋様を表現し、線の太さが均等であるため、力強く、形は「屈鉄盤糸」のようであるから「鉄線描」と呼ばれる。このような描き方は唐代になって大いに発展し、代表的な作品として閻立本の『歴代帝王図』がある。そこでは、王の服及び髭は全て鉄線で描き、真に迫った最上の作品と言える。唐代の墓室にある壁画、特に石棺と石槨の石刻線画にも常に「鉄線描き」が使われた。永泰公主墓を例とすれば、その石槨に彫刻された宮女は団扇を握ったり、玉盤を捧げ持ったり、嫁入り道具を取ったり、弁当箱を抱えたり、燭台をあげたりして、しとやかな立ち居振る舞いで温和な容貌をしており、その容姿は卓越しており、その造形は優美である。侍女が履くロングスカートは鉄線で描かれたものが多く、円盤に載せた糸のように円く、非常に軽妙で、石刻侍女画の傑作と思われる。「蘭葉描」の特徴は線形の変化が多種多様なので、圧力も均等ではなく、筆の使い方は粗かったり細かったりして、形は蘭葉のようだから、「蘭葉描」と称される。聞くところによると、このような描き方は唐代の大画家の呉道子によって創立されたものである。彼は常にその方法で人物を描写し、線の筆致が自由奔放であることから、「呉帯当風（呉は当風を帯びる）」と言い伝えられている。

[9]陳授祥（2001）『隋唐絵画史』人民美術出版社。

唐代絵画の重要な構成部分である乾陵陪葬墓の石刻線画は、線を主要な表現技法としている。その手法は伝統的な中国画の線描の手法ときわめて似ている。ただし、乾陵陪葬墓の石刻線画は地味な線で画面を構築して、線の造形で絵を彫刻した作品である。石刻線画の特徴は石材を媒体にし、刀を筆として、線で絵を描くことである。そのため、その作品は絵画と彫塑の二重の性質を持つ。従って、ただ絵画芸術をよく知るのみならず、さらに彫刻の技巧を熟知する人が石刻線刻画の仕事を完成させることができる。乾陵陪葬墓の石刻線刻画より見ると、当時の画家は線の運用に熟練にしており、複雑な内容を表現することができ、また彫刻者も線と物の形の緊密な連絡の中から、線の太さ、軽重、力度、質感、起伏、リズム、変化などを表現することができる。単純にすべきところを単純にし、複雑なところを複雑にし、境を以て線を描き、意を以て線を描き、それによって優れた趣が次々とあふれ出て、自然を超越するような境地に達する。

五

乾陵陪葬墓石刻線画は芸術作品であるだけではなく、同時に重要な歴史的価値を有する文物でもある。そこには唐代前期の著名な画工と彫刻家の真跡が保存されている。それは我々に歴史や文化に関する多くの重要な情報を与えてくれる。

第一に、乾陵陪葬墓石刻線画の研究は唐代絵画研究の重要な基礎部分である。唐代は我が国の絵画芸術が勢いよく発展する時代であった。唐代289年間、閻立本兄弟、尉遅親子、李将軍親子、王維、呉道玄など有名な画家がたくさん現れた。彼らは唐代の歴史上で活躍し、数多くの傑作を作り出した。しかしながら、年代が古いのにくわえ、自然的あるいは人為的破壊により大多数の作品が消滅した。乾陵陪葬墓石刻線画は墓葬等級の高い陪葬墓に入れられたため幸いにして難を逃れ、ほぼ完全な形で発見された。さらに重要なのは、乾陵陪葬墓石刻線画の数量が多く内容も豊富で水準が高いことである。乾陵陪葬墓石刻線画は唐代石刻芸術の傑作であり、唐代絵画芸術の宝でもある、唐人が我々に与えた貴重な文化遺産だと言っても過言ではない。

第二に、乾陵陪葬墓石刻線画は唐の文化を理解するための重要な資料である。唐代は中国古代文化が最も輝いた時代の一つである。乾陵陪葬墓石刻線画は唐代石刻芸術の宝として、その芸術的な魅力を示すと同時に、当時の社会生活を活写した絵巻物であり、唐代史研究における貴重な資料である。石刻線画の題材は侍女の絵が多数を占める。彼女たちの服飾には、短い上着、肩掛け、ロングスカート、雲頭鞋・線鞋・細い袖丸い襟の長衣・折り襟の長衣・ストライプのズボンなどがあり、髪型には単螺髻・双螺髻・単刀髻・蝶形髻などの種類があり、頭髪を飾る各種類の簪には歩揺・珠花などがある。それらは唐代文化研究にとって、最も優れた実物資料であり、文献記録の欠を補うものである。そのうえ、唐代の服飾の発展と変遷の研究にも積極的な意味を持つものである。石刻線画は石椁を装飾するものであるが、墓主の身分と栄誉の象徴であるだけでなく、墓主の宮廷生活を展示し、かつ当時の喪葬制度も反映されている。これらは唐代史の研究に貴重な資料を提供してくれるのである。

第三に、乾陵陪葬墓石刻線画は唐の生態環境の研究にも役立つ。文献史料によれば、唐人は花鳥を好むという。石刻線画にもいろいろな種類の花木が見える。例えば、木は槿・石楠・モ

[1]李傑（2011）「唐代石椁人物的線刻芸術」『美術』11、p.103。

チノキ・クチナシなどが描かれる。花はチューリ
ップ・ゆり・ヤブミョガ・金盞花・草菊など、鳥は
オシドリ・雲雀・七面鳥・青鳥・百霊・伯労・鶯・
ツバメなど十何種類もある。昆虫はトンボ・蝶・
蜂などがある。花の組み合わせ、構図、模様や点
と面の結び合わせが絶妙である。

　例えば、章懐太子墓石槨の内部の柱には、
纏枝巻葉・纏枝海石榴・巻葉裏荷・巻葉海石榴
・大葉海石榴などが描かれており、その中でも
纏枝海石榴が多数を占める。そのほか、墓室の
廡殿門南窓の上の部分に二匹の馬が向き合っ
て疾駆し、その間に二つの巻葉紋が描かれてい
る。中央部は直櫺窓のまわりを草葉紋で飾って
いる。下の部分は二頭のトラが向かい合って立
ち、草葉紋をもってその間を隔て、トラの周囲を
巻葉紋で装飾している。槨の外の象徴的な殿門
の上には巻葉海石榴の紋と二匹の鳳凰（尾の部
分が海石榴）があり、まわりも海石榴紋で飾って
いる。

　永泰公主墓の石門と石槨もそのような紋様
が多い。一つ一つの石刻線画の周囲を飾り、絵
画を場面ごとに区切ることで、各々を相対的に一
幅の絵画として独立させている。例えば、石槨の
外部の東壁に「直櫺窓図」がある。その上部分
には巻雲紋があり、二匹の鳳凰が向き合って踊
っている。中央の部分は巻葉海石榴を飾ってい
る。下の部分は二頭の獅子が向き合って立ち、
二頭の間を抱合式巻草図で相隔て、下部を巻葉
紋で装飾している。その動物と植物は唐人の美
意識を表現するだけでなく、ある程度は唐前期
の生態環境が反映されているのである。

　石刻線画は石刻芸術の一種であり、民族文
化の長い歴史に重要な地位を占め、世界の美術
史にも独特の位置を占める。ある学者は次のよう
に考えている。「唐の石槨線刻は、絵画を基準と
して石材の特徴に応じて筆の代わりに刀を使い、

石に刻んで輪郭を取り、独特な芸術的風格を備
えている。その刻石技法は、漢代の漢画像石より
発展したが、漢代の漢画像石はまだ彫塑的な技
法の範疇にある。しかしながら、唐代石槨線刻の
刻石技法は絵画の毛筆の使用法と基本的に一致
しており、その属性は彫塑よりも絵画に近い。彫
刻刀の使い方や刃の形の変化と石刻線画の造形
と塑像は、みな絵画の様式変遷に従って変化し
た。唐代の石刻線画の刻石技法の変遷は、三段
階に分けて考えることができる。一つは魏晋南北
朝の刻石技法を継承した魏晋遺刀時期（630-
689）、二つ目は絵画の線形を模倣した刀似絵時
期（706-721）、三つ目は本体の特性に注意し筆
の代わりに刀を使用した時期（724-748）であ
る。[10]」乾陵陪葬墓石刻線画はその第二段階に属
し、中国絵画史の過去の成果を受け継ぎ、新たな
道を切り開く役割を果たした。宋代と元代の石刻
線画は衰退の傾向があったが、重要な作品もいく
つかある。例えば、宋代の『水陸斎戒儀神像図』
は主題によって三つ部分に分けられ、天国と地獄
の十八柱の神を描いており、神々の何れも、修真
度世の姿を備えているのである。元代の『朝元仙
仗図』、『玄宗問法図』も宗教的な石刻線画の傑
作である。明清時期は理学が盛んで、親孝行を表
現した作品が多かったが、その内容と技術はすべ
て唐代の石刻線画に多かれ少なかれ影響を受け
ている。以上より考えると、唐代の石刻線画が、
中国絵画史の重要な地位を占めていることは十
分明らかであろう。

第二幅

拓片（135cm×34cm,0.4590m²）

线描（135cm×34cm,0.4590m²）

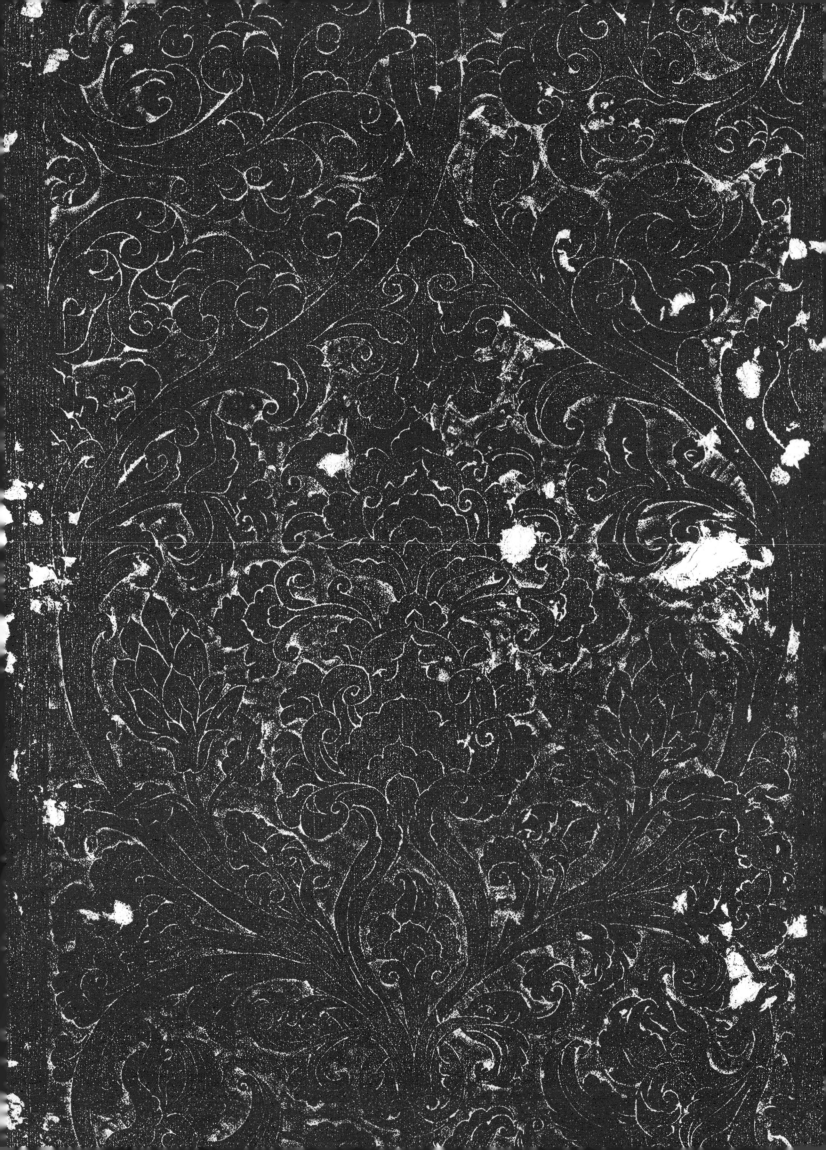

第三幅

拓片（133.5cm×34cm,0.4539m²）

线描（133.5cm×34cm,0.4539m²）

第四幅

拓片（137cm×34cm，0.4658m²）

线描（137cm×34cm，0.4658m²）

第五幅

拓片（136cm×33cm,0.4488m²）

线描（136cm×33cm,0.4488m²）

第六幅

拓片（133cm×33cm,0.4389m²）

线描（133cm×33cm,0.4389m²）

第七幅

拓片（137cm×34cm, 0.4658m²）

线描（137cm×34cm, 0.4658m²）

第八幅

拓片（138cm×30cm,0.4140m²）
线描（138cm×30cm,0.4140m²）

第九幅

拓片（134cm×35cm,0.4690m²）

线描（134cm×35cm,0.4690m²）

第十幅

拓片（136cm×33.5cm,0.4556m²）

线描（136cm×33.5cm,0.4556m²）

第十一幅

拓片（135cm×35.5cm,0.4793m²）

线描（135cm×35.5cm,0.4793m²）

第十二幅

拓片（138cm×34cm,0.4692m²）

线描（138cm×34cm,0.4692m²）

第十三幅

拓片（136cm×31cm,0.4216m²）

线描（136cm×31cm,0.4216m²）

第十四幅

拓片（138cm×36cm, 0.4968m²）

线描（138cm×36cm, 0.4968m²）

第一幅

拓片（131cm×81cm,1.0611m²）

第二幅

线描（131cm×81cm,1.0611m²）

第二幅

拓片（130cm×75cm,0.9750m²）

第二幅

线描（130cm×75cm,0.9750m²）

第三幅

拓片（132cm×67cm,0.8844m²）

第三幅

线描（132cm×67cm,0.8844m²）

074

第一编
线条艺术的遗产
唐乾陵陪葬墓石椁线刻画

第四幅

拓片（131cm×80cm,1.0480m²）

第四幅

线描（131cm×80cm,1.0480m²）

第五幅

拓片（132cm×63cm,0.8316m²）

第五幅

线描（132cm×63cm,0.8316m²）

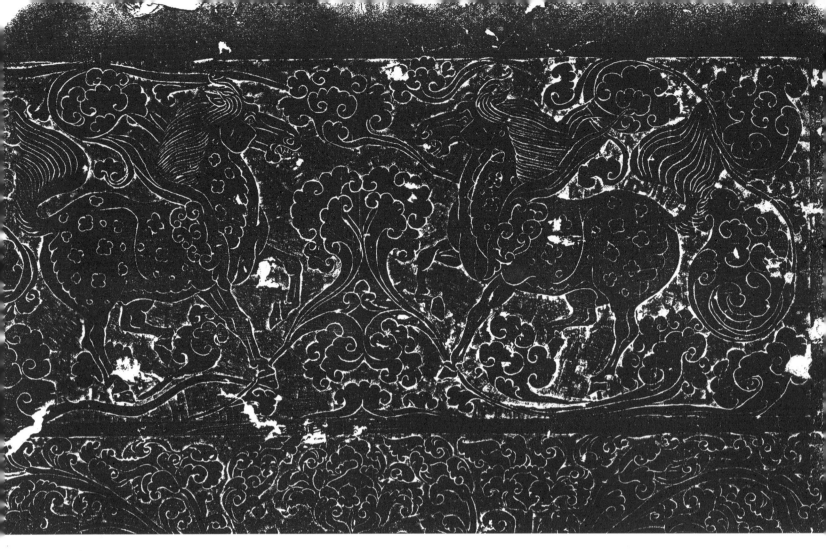

拓片局部

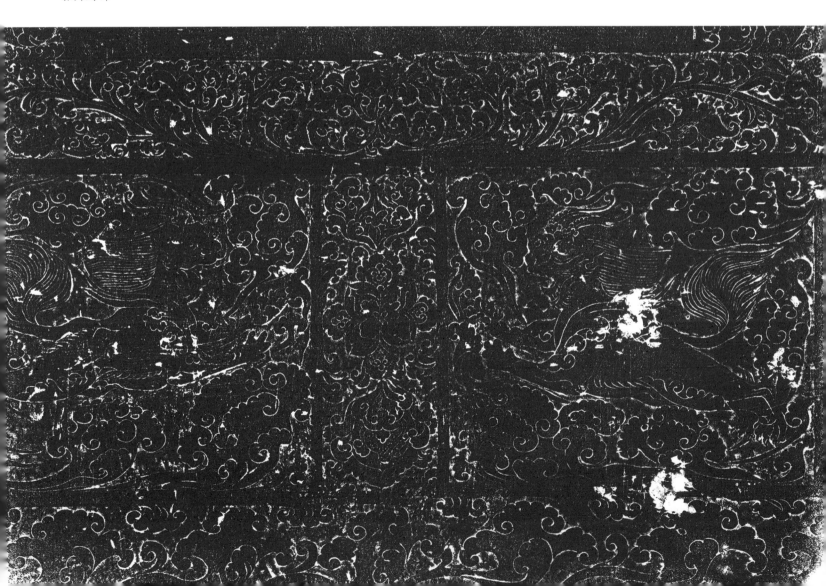

线描局部

第六幅

拓片（127cm×74cm,0.9398m²）

第六幅

线描（127cm×74cm,0.9398m²）

第七幅

拓片（128cm×81cm, 1.0368m²）

第七幅

线描（128cm×81cm,1.0368m²）

第八幅

拓片（132cm×74cm,0.9768m²）

第八幅

线描（132cm×74cm,0.9768m²）

第九幅

线描（130cm×68cm,0.8840m²）

第十幅

拓片（133cm×69cm,0.9177m²）

第十幅

线描（133cm×69cm,0.9177m²）

第一幅

拓片（136cm×35cm）

线描（0.4760m²）

第二幅

拓片（137cm×33cm）

线描（0.4521m²）

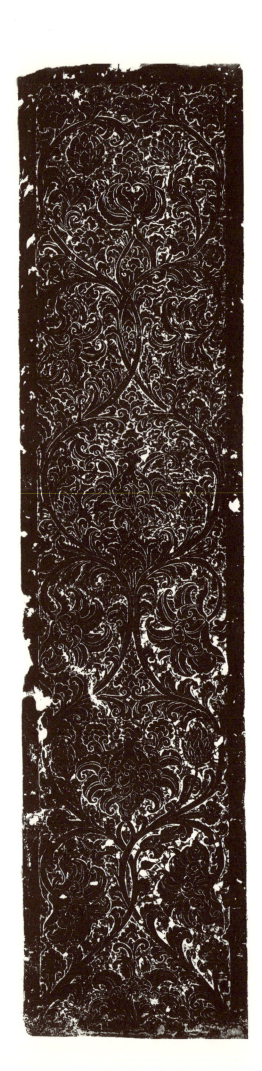

第三幅

拓片（135cm×32cm）

线描（0.4320m²）

第四幅

拓片（136cm×35cm）

线描（0.4760m²）

第五幅

拓片（137cm×34cm）

线描（0.4658m²）

第六幅

拓片（136cm×30cm）

线描（0.4080m²）

第一幅

拓片（126cm×80cm,1.0080m²）

第一幅

线描（126cm×80cm,1.0080m²）

第二幅

线描（128cm×75cm，0.9600m²）

第三幅

第三幅

线描（131cm×69cm,0.9039m²）

第四幅

拓片（130cm×81cm, 1.0530m²）

第四幅

线描（130cm×81cm，1.0530m²）

第五幅

拓片（130cm×68cm,0.8840m²）

第五幅

线描（130cm×68cm,0.8840m²）

第六幅

拓片（125cm×79cm,0.9875m²）

第六幅

线描（125cm×79cm,0.9875m²）

第七幅

拓片（125cm×83cm，1.0375m²）

第七幅

线描（125cm×83cm,1.0375m²）

拓片（125cm×74cm,0.9250m²）

第八幅

线描（125cm×74cm,0.9250m²）

112

第九幅

拓片（124cm×67cm,0.8308m²）

第九幅

线描（124cm×67cm,0.8308m²）

第十幅

拓片（124cm×73cm,0.9052m²）

第十幅

线描（124cm×73cm,0.9052m²）

仕 女

内壁第七幅
内壁第三幅

仆 从

外壁第四幅
内壁第九幅

鸟

内壁第十幅
内壁第九幅
外壁第一幅
外壁第四幅

兽

外壁第三幅
外壁第五幅
外壁第三幅

花卉

外壁第八幅

内壁第二幅

内壁第八幅

内壁第一幅

蔓草

外柱第八幅
外柱第七幅
内柱第六幅
内柱第五幅

第二幅

拓片（134cm×34cm,0.4556m²）

线描（134cm×34cm,0.4556m²）

第三幅

拓片（134.5cm×34.5cm, 0.4640m²）

线描（134.5cm×34.5cm, 0.4640m²）

第四幅

拓片（134cm×34.3cm,0.4596m²）

线描（134cm×34.3cm,0.4596m²）

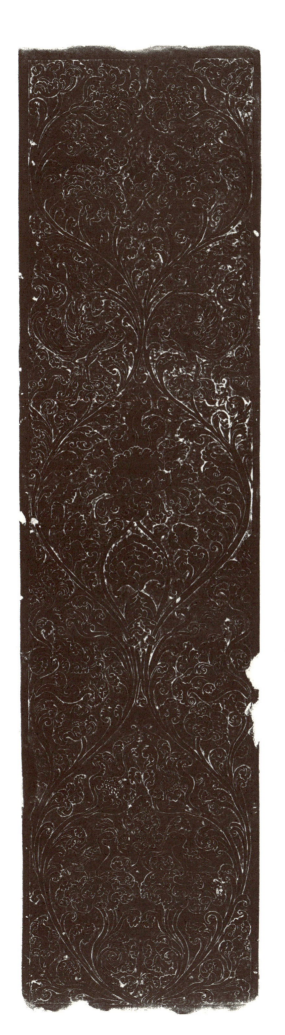

第五幅

拓片（134cm×34.5cm,0.4623m²）

线描（134cm×34.5cm,0.4623m²）

第六幅

拓片（135cm×35cm,0.4725m²）

线描（135cm×35cm,0.4725m²）

第七幅

拓片（134cm×30.5cm, 0.4087m²）

线描（134cm×30.5cm, 0.4087m²）

第八幅

拓片（134cm×34cm,0.4556m²）

线描（134cm×34cm,0.4556m²）

第九幅

拓片（134cm×35cm, 0.4690m²）

线描（134cm×35cm, 0.4690m²）

第十幅

拓片（135cm×34cm,0.4590m²）

线描（135cm×34cm,0.4590m²）

第一幅

拓片（130cm×80.5cm,1.0465m²）

第一幅

线描（130cm×80.5cm,1.0465m²）

第二幅

拓片（129cm×79cm,1.0191m²）

第二幅

线描（129cm×79cm,1.0191m²）

第三幅

拓片（136.5cm×67cm, 0.9146m²）

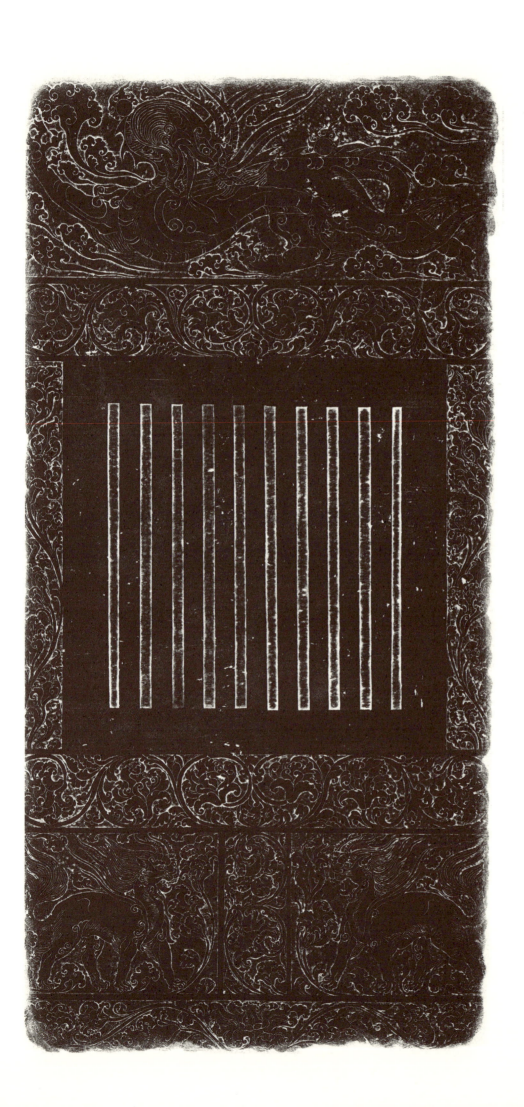

第三幅

线描（136.5cm×67cm,0.9146m²）

第四幅

拓片（133.5cm×75.5cm，1.0079m²）

第四幅

线描（133.5cm×75.5cm,1.0079m²）

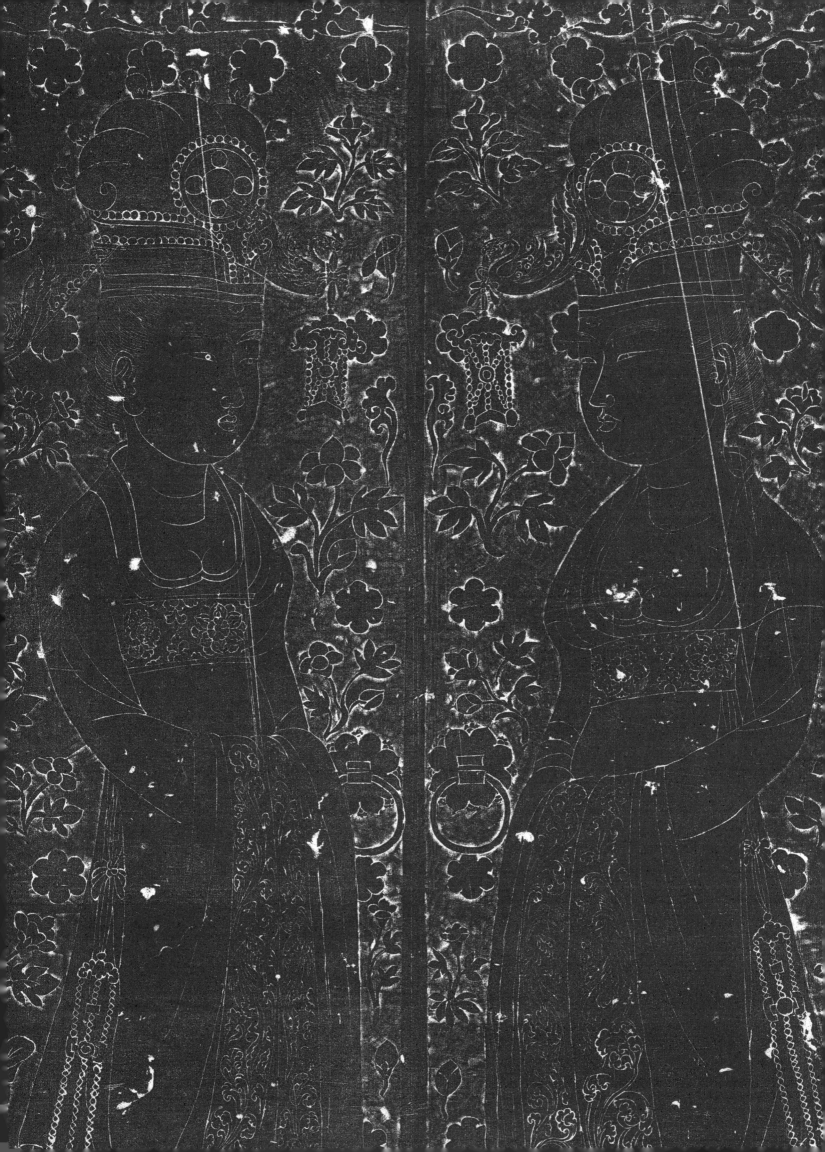

第五幅

拓片（133.5cm×69.5cm,0.9278m²）

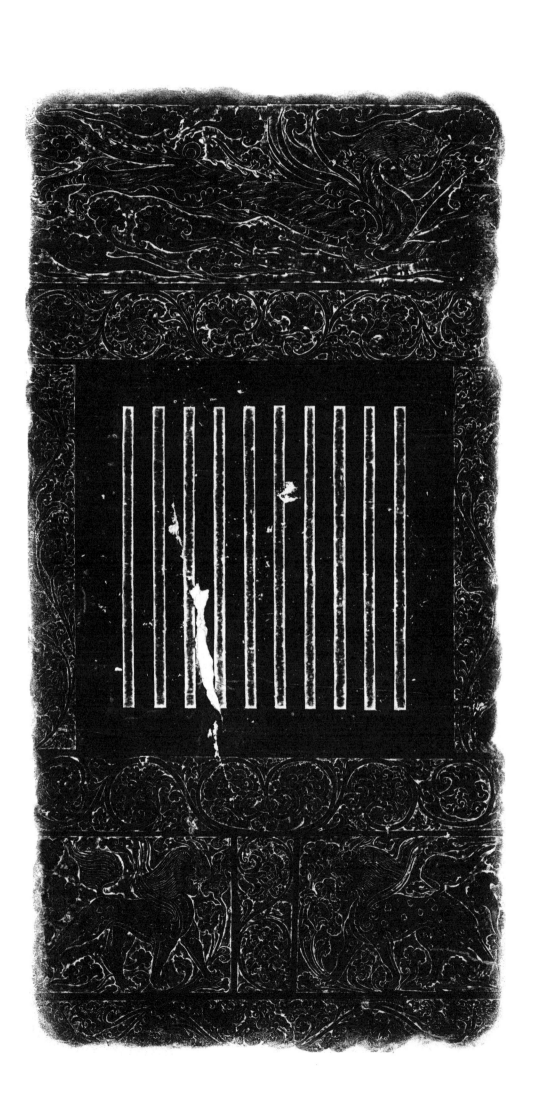

第五幅

线描（133.5cm×69.5cm,0.9278m²）

第六幅

拓片（131.5cm×80cm,1.0520m²）

第六幅

线描（131.5cm×80cm,1.0520m²）

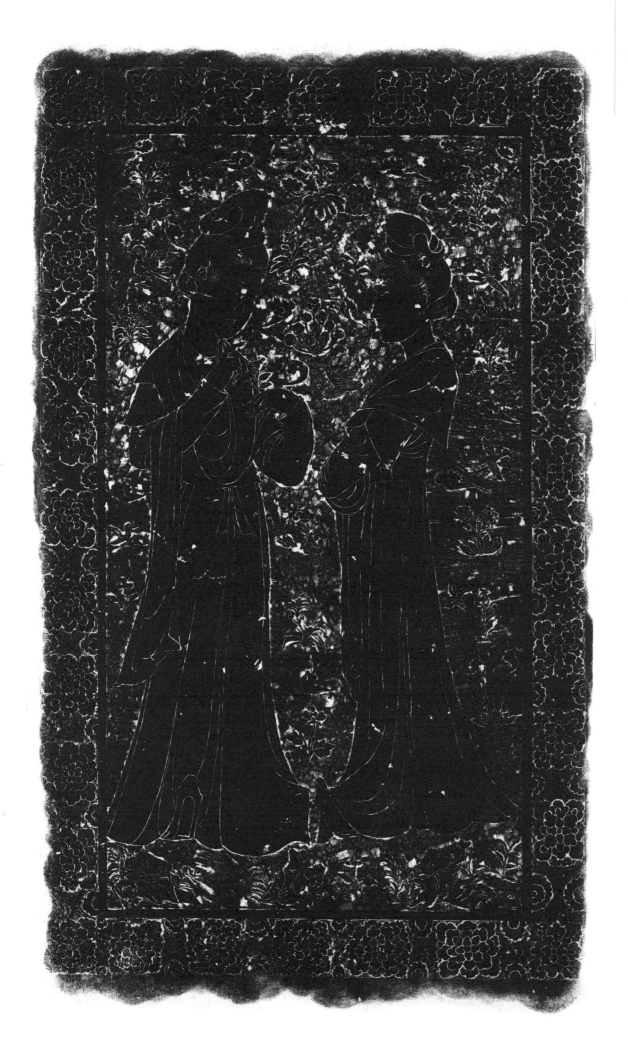

第七幅

线描（130cm×80cm,1.0400m²）

第一幅

拓片（133cm×34cm）

线描（0.4522m²）

第二幅

拓片（134cm×34cm）

线描（0.4556m²）

第三幅

拓片（134cm×34cm）

线描（0.4556m²）

第四幅

拓片（133.5cm×33cm）

线描（0.4406m²）

第五幅

拓片（133.5cm×34cm）

线描（0.4539m²）

第六幅

拓片（134cm×34cm）

线描（0.4556m²）

第一幅

拓片（131cm×80cm,1.0480m²）

第一幅

线描（131cm×80cm,1.0480m²）

第二幅

拓片（130.5cm×79cm,1.0310m²）

第二幅

线描（130.5cm×79cm,1.0310m²）

第三幅

线描（127.5cm×68cm,0.8670m²）

第四幅

拓片（128cm×74cm,0.9472m²）

第四幅

线描（128cm×74cm,0.9472m²）

第五幅

拓片（129cm×68.5cm,0.8837m²）

第五幅

线描（129cm×68.5cm，0.8837m²）

第六幅

线描（131cm×80cm,1.0480m²）

第七幅

拓片（131.5cm×80.5cm,1.0586m²）

第七幅

线描（131.5cm×80.5cm,1.0586m²）

第八幅

拓片（131cm×66cm,0.8646m²）

第八幅

线描（131cm×66cm,0.8646m²）

第九幅

拓片（129cm×72cm,0.9288m²）

第九幅

线描（129cm×72cm,0.9288m²）

第十幅

拓片（129cm×68cm,0.8772m²）

第十幅

线描（129cm×68cm,0.8772m²）

仕 女

外壁第四幅

仕 女

内壁第三幅

仆 从

外壁第一幅

仆 从

内壁第九幅

鸟

外柱第六幅
外壁第七幅
内柱第二幅
外柱第一幅

兽

内柱第六幅
内柱第五幅
外壁第五幅

兽

外壁第三幅

花 卉

外壁第六幅
外壁第六幅
外壁第七幅
外壁第七幅
内壁第六幅
内壁第二幅
内柱第五幅
内柱第一幅

蔓　草

外壁第四幅
外壁第四幅
内壁第四幅
内壁第四幅

外壁第三幅
外壁第四幅

蔓草

外壁第四幅

鸟

内壁第十幅
内壁第九幅
外壁第一幅
外壁第四幅

线条艺术的遗产
唐乾陵陪葬墓石椁线刻画

兽

外壁第五幅
外壁第三幅

兽

外壁第三幅

花 卉

外壁第八幅
内壁第二幅
内壁第八幅
内壁第一幅

蔓草

外柱第八幅
外柱第七幅
内柱第六幅
内柱第五幅

第二幅

拓片（134.5cm×35cm,0.4708m²）

线描（134.5cm×35cm,0.4708m²）

第三幅

拓片（135cm×35cm,0.4725m²）

线描（135cm×35cm,0.4725m²）

第四幅

拓片（135cm×35cm,0.4725m²）

线描（135cm×35cm,0.4725m²）

第五幅

拓片（134cm×35.5cm,0.4757m²）

线描（134cm×35.5cm,0.4757m²）

第六幅

拓片（134cm×35cm,0.4690m²）

线描（134cm×35cm,0.4690m²）

第七幅

拓片（134cm×33.5cm,0.4489m²）

线描（134cm×33.5cm,0.4489m²）

第八幅

拓片（136cm×33.5cm,0.4556m²）

线描（136cm×33.5cm,0.4556m²）

第九幅

拓片（136cm×35.5cm,0.4828m²）

线描（136cm×35.5cm,0.4828m²）

第十幅

拓片（134cm×34.5cm，0.4623m²）

线描（134cm×34.5cm，0.4623m²）

第一幅

线描（136.5cm×76.5cm,1.0442m²）

第二幅

线描（137cm×80cm,1.0960m²）

第三幅

拓片（136.5cm×68.5cm,0.9350m²）

第三幅

线描（136.5cm×68.5cm,0.9350m²）

第四幅

拓片（136cm×80cm,1.0880m²）

第四幅

线描（136cm×80cm,1.0880m²）

第五幅

拓片（136cm×66cm,0.8976m²）

第五幅

线描（136cm×66cm,0.8976m²）

第六幅

拓片（136cm×77.5cm,1.0540m²）

第六幅

线描（136cm×77.5cm,1.0540m²）

第三编
线条艺术的遗产
唐乾陵陪葬墓石椁线刻画

232

第七幅

拓片（136cm×76.5cm,1.0404m²）

第七幅

线描（136cm×76.5cm，1.0404m²）

第一幅

拓片（132cm×35cm,0.4620m²）

线描（132cm×35cm,0.4620m²）

第二幅

拓片（131.5cm×35.5cm,0.4668m²）

线描（131.5cm×35.5cm,0.4668m²）

第三幅

拓片（132.5cm×35.5cm,0.4704m²）

线描（132.5cm×35.5cm,0.4704m²）

第四幅

拓片（133.5cm×35.3cm, 0.4713m²）

线描（133.5cm×35.3cm, 0.4713m²）

第五幅

拓片（133cm×35.5cm,0.4722m²）

线描（133cm×35.5cm,0.4722m²）

第六幅

拓片（132.5cm×35cm,0.4638m²）

线描（132.5cm×35cm,0.4638m²）

第一幅

拓片（131.5cm×76.5cm,1.0060m²）

第一幅

线描（131.5cm×76.5cm，1.0060m²）

第二幅

拓片（134.5cm×80cm,1.0760m²）

第二幅

线描（134.5cm×80cm,1.0760m²）

第三幅

拓片（135cm×67.5cm,0.9113m²）

第三幅

线描（135cm×67.5cm,0.9113m²）

第四幅

拓片（130.5cm×79cm,1.0310m²）

第四幅

线描（130.5cm×79cm，1.0310m²）

第五幅

拓片（132.5cm×66cm,0.8745m²）

第五幅

线描（132.5cm×66cm,0.8745m²）

第六幅

拓片（130.5cm×78cm,1.0179m²）

第六幅

线描（130.5cm×78cm,1.0179m²）

第七幅

拓片（130.5cm×76cm,0.9918m²）

第七幅

线描（130.5cm×76cm,0.9918m²）

第八幅

线描（135.5cm×76cm，1.0298m²）

第九幅

拓片（130.5cm×78cm,1.0179m²）

第九幅

线描（130.5cm×78cm,1.0179m²）

第十幅

拓片（136cm×68.5cm,0.9316m²）

第十幅

线描（136cm×68.5cm, 0.9316m²）

仕 女

内壁第四幅

仆 从

内壁第一幅
内壁第五幅

仕 女

仆 从

外壁第七幅
内壁第七幅

鸟

内壁第十幅
内壁第七幅
内柱第六幅
外柱第六幅
外壁第五幅

鸟

兽

外柱第六幅
外柱第五幅

花卉

外壁第六幅
外壁第二幅
内壁第二幅
内壁第一幅

蔓草

外柱第七幅
内柱第一幅
外柱第八幅

乾陵线刻画内容丰富，异常精美，是唐代给我们留下的宝贵财富。数十年来，我们一直有一个愿望，想把这些线刻画整理出来，呈现给大家。当我们编好此书时，内心由衷感到欣慰。

在编写本书的过程中，我们的心情是复杂的。一方面常常被博大精深的唐代艺术所感染，另一方面也常常感到自己力不从心，担心自己不能很好地把唐代线刻艺术表现出来。好在我们具有得天独厚的条件，经过几年时间的努力，终于完成了这项艰巨的任务。

本书在编纂过程中，得到了乾陵博物馆副馆长刘向阳、馆长助理王晓莉、行政办公室副主任兼信息中心主任曾小琦、资料研究室主任侯晓斌、陈列保管部主任宋少宇、副主任张鑫的倾心关注和帮助，多次共同研究和探讨书中的相关问题；乾陵管理处团委书记、摄影师田园同志为本书拍摄了很好的照片；业务部门的魏鹏、李阿能同志逐一核对线刻画，确保线刻画的准确性；穆兴平、郑勋、李青峰、赵维娜、杨麦娟同志反复实地丈量线刻画的尺寸和记录位置；吕涛、李育红同志为本书做了不少辅助工作；信息中心的刘艳同志为本书的电子版制作做了大量的工作；文物出版社的总编辑葛承雍教授和责任编辑李睿副编审也为本书印制出版和设计策划付出了大量的劳动。在此一并表示谢忱！

编者

2012. 12. 27

图书在版编目（ＣＩＰ）数据

线条艺术的遗产：唐乾陵陪葬墓石椁线刻画 / 樊英峰，王双怀编著. -- 北京：文物出版社，2013.6 （2016.6重印）

ISBN 978-7-5010-3719-3

Ⅰ.①线… Ⅱ.①樊… ②王… Ⅲ.①唐墓-墓室壁画-乾县-图录 Ⅳ.①K879.412

中国版本图书馆CIP数据核字(2013)第104406号

线条艺术的遗产：唐乾陵陪葬墓石椁线刻画

编 著 者：樊英峰　王双怀

责任编辑：李　睿
责任印制：梁秋卉
装帧设计：雅昌设计中心·北京 田之友

出版发行：文物出版社
社　　址：北京东直门内北小街2号楼
邮　　编：100007
网　　址：http://www.wenwu.com
邮　　箱：web@wenwu.com
印　　刷：文物出版社印刷厂
开　　本：635×965毫米　1/16
印　　张：17
版　　次：2013年6月第1版
印　　次：2016年6月第2次印刷
书　　号：ISBN 978-7-5010-3719-3
定　　价：280.00元